ANNUAL 2007
Bologna

L'Autore della Copertina

Cover Illustration by

Wolf Erlbruch

Come fa una storia semplice a diventare un libro grandioso

Chiunque abbia a che fare con i libri illustrati conosce bene il problema: un libro o piace agli adulti o piace ai ragazzi, è raro che piaccia ad entrambi. Wolf Erlbruch è uno dei pochi illustratori che riesca a soddisfare i lettori adulti riuscendo allo stesso tempo ad intrattenere i più giovani. Quando l'editore tedesco Peter Hammer Verlag chiese a Erlbruch di illustrare una storia dello scrittore ghanese James Aggrey, egli lo fece seguendo quelle che credeva fossero le aspettative per un libro illustrato. Fino a quel momento, Erlbruch aveva avuto successo nella pubblicità, lavorando per riviste come *Playboy, Esquire* e il settimanale tedesco *Stern*. Sapeva esattamente come soddisfare le aspettative del pubblico. Quel libro *Der Adler, der nicht fliegen wollte* ne fu la prova: le illustrazioni erano leggere ed eteree, senza traccia dell'Erlbruch che conosciamo adesso. Vent'anni dopo, troviamo una serie di elementi che ci siamo abituati ad associare immediatamente ad Erlbruch: la carta a quadretti tipo quaderno di matematica, la carta verde che ricorda la parete di una cucina, le mappe topografiche, gli stampini di gomma, gli animali ritagliati dalle enciclopedie illustrate. Il materiale è usato in modo così parsimonioso che c'è spazio e tempo per vedere, per recepire sia il contenuto che la sostanza. Questi sono gli ingredienti più amati di Erlbruch rielaborati ogni volta in modo diverso.

Ripercorrendo le tappe del suo lavoro, se sfogliamo *Chi me l'ha fatta in testa,* il libro illustrato nel 1989 dopo una lunga pausa e tratto dalla storia di Werner Holzwarth, è già riconoscibile come un "Erlbruch". Una mattina, una piccola talpa si sveglia e scopre che qualcuno gliela fatta in testa. La talpa vaga, con un atteggiamento di rimprovero, nelle diverse immagini, esaminando i "bisognini" dei sospettati.
L'animaletto porta l'oggetto incriminato sulla testa come un turbante: è una caricatura ma, come l'opera del caricaturista norvegese Gulbransson, è disegnata amorevolmente, con personalità. Questo è dovuto in parte alle figure, delineate e colorate a pennarello che si muovono attraverso uno sfondo pallido, come attori su un palcoscenico. Fanno parte dello stile di Erlbruch proprio come l'improvvisa comparsa di una mucca dall'aspetto realistico in mezzo agli altri bizzarri personaggi. Nel 1990, con la pubblicazione del secondo libro illustrato di Erlbruch *I terribili cinque*, storia di cinque emarginati che riacquistano stima e credibilità nel loro ambiente ritrovandosi abitualmente sulla spiaggia, si aggiungono varie componenti nuove alla mitologia personale di Erlbruch: la luna onnipresente che illumina i suoi disegni dall'atmosfera malinconica, la passione per la musica *offbeat*, l'attenzione per gli aspetti tipografici e l'attenta progettazione delle ultime pagine. Si tratta del primo libro scritto dallo stesso Erlbruch che conferisce alla storia un particolare senso dell'umorismo e lo rende così autentico. Il libro successivo pubblicato l'anno seguente, è altrettanto avvincente ed arguto. Si intitola *Leonard* dal nome di un ragazzino con la fobia dei cani, ispirato al figlio di Erlbruch, Leo. Infatti i personaggi della storia corrispondono ai componenti

Letter "I". Bambi / cotelett-head

Letter "V".
Innuit looking at a clock

Letter "Q".
Man drinking from same pond as deer

di tutta la famiglia, compresa la nonna di Leonard, che va in giro a quattro zampe con un osso in bocca. Perché lo fa? Per far passare la paura dei cani a Leonard. Le pagine finali sono illustrate dallo stesso Leo. Al tempo della pubblicazione, Erlbruch ha commentato: "Leo ha continuato a disegnare cani dall'aspetto pauroso finché, ad un certo punto, non ne ha più avuto paura". Questa è una delle funzioni dell'arte. Il seguito della saga familiare che risale al 1995, *La Signora Meier e il merlo*, ha la stessa genialità. Tutto è presente nella stessa misura: sfondo autobiografico, i dettagli dell'opera artistica, il riferimento alla storia dell'arte e, cosa più importante di tutte, la storia.

Qui arriviamo al mio libro preferito, *La notte* dove l'essenza di ogni illustrazione (il modo in cui il mondo del testo si rispecchia e viene trasformato in immagini) diventa il tema e il principio guida del libro. Siamo nel mezzo della notte e il piccolo Fons non riesce a dormire, così sveglia il padre e insieme cominciano a camminare per la città immersa nel buio. E mentre attorno a loro succedono le cose più strane, il padre cammina tenendo il figlio per mano, trascinando i piedi, gli occhi semichiusi, e dice che tutti dormono e che non c'è nulla da vedere. Egli non si accorge che c'è un pesce che spinge una fragola in un passeggino, che il ponte in realtà è il dorso di un cane, e che un gorilla ha dato una mano a suo figlio… non vede assolutamente nulla! Alla fine del libro il padre si rimette sotto le coperte, perché naturalmente di notte non succede niente: "è solo buio". Questo libro delizioso può essere letto come una riprova della distanza tra il mondo dei bambini e quello degli adulti. Ecco uno dei maggiori punti di forza di Erlbruch: dipingere i bambini nel mondo degli adulti e gli adulti nel mondo dei bambini. I due mondi coesistono affiancati, senza che nessuno dei due prevalga rispetto all'altro. Bambini e adulti si sorridono con reciproca tenerezza, simpatia e forse anche con un poco di irritazione. Per questo, meglio farsi valere lealmente, parlando ognuno per sé, come fra padre e figlio o, ne *La creazione*, come fra Dio e l'uomo. In questo modo, tutti sono contenti e nessuno ci rimette.

Poi naturalmente ci sono tutti gli altri libri illustrati da Erlbruch: le sue immagini per *La fabbrica delle farfalle* di Gioconda Belli, la sua versione di *Das Hexeneinmaleins* di Goethe, e la sua splendida reinterpretazione del *Neues ABC-Buch* di Karl Philipp Moritz. Queste illustrazioni meriterebbero di venir esposte alle pareti di una galleria d'arte: per gli amanti dell'arte rappresentano una vera delizia. Eppure, sono altri per me i libri più commoventi. Niente avventure, niente problemi sociali e niente eroi, solo semplici storie. Come quella sul non riuscire a dormire la notte, sulla morte del nonno, sul volere qualcuno da abbracciare, sul prendersi cura di un uccellino che non può volare. Oppure, sull'alzarsi tutti i giorni e dover creare un altro pezzetto di mondo. Solo semplici storie che diventano libri grandiosi.

Konrad Heidkamp
Redattore esperto in libri per ragazzi per *Die Zeit*

How Simples Stories Become Great Books

Anyone who has anything to do with picture books will know the problem: either adults like them, or children like them, but seldom both. Wolf Erlbruch is one of the few illustrators to succeed in satisfying the big readers while keeping the little ones entertained. When German publishers Peter Hammer Verlag asked Wolf Erlbruch to illustrate a story by the Ghanaian writer James Aggrey, Erlbruch drew his pictures the way he thought people expected picture books to look. Until then he'd had a successful career in advertising, illustrating for Playboy, Esquire *and the German weekly* Stern. *He knew exactly how to satisfy people's expectations. The resulting picture book* The Eagle That Would Not Fly *demonstrates as much: the illustrations are light and insubstantial. There's no evidence of Erlbruch as we know him.*

Twenty years on and there are a number of ingredients that we've come to associate with Erlbruch: the squared maths-book-style paper, the green kitchen-wall-like paper, the topographical maps, the rubber stamps, the animals cut out of picture encyclopaedias. The material is used so sparingly that there's space and time to see, to take in both content and substance. These are much-loved Erlbruch recipes that have been served up many times.

Looking back, if you flick through the book that he illustrated in 1989 after a long pause from a Werner Holzwarth's story, The Story of the Little Mole Who Knew It Was None of His Business, *you can already identify it as an 'Erlbruch'. One morning the little mole wakes up to find someone has 'done its business' on his head. He wanders reproachfully through the pictures, investigating the waste products of all the likely suspects. The mole carries the offending article on his head like a turban: he's a caricature, but - like the artwork of Norwegian caricaturist Gulbransson - drawn lovingly and with individuality. This is due in part to the figures — felt-tip coloured cut-outs that move across pale backgrounds like actors on a stage. They're as much a part of Erlbruch's style as the sudden appearance of a realistic-looking cow in amidst the other quirky characters.*

With the publication of Erlbruch's second picture book of 1990, The Terrible Five - *the story of five social outcasts who win back their street cred by hanging out together at the beach - a number of new components were added to Erlbruch's personal mythology: the ever-present moon that illuminates his dusky drawings, his love of offbeat music, his attention to typography, and the careful design of the end-papers. Moreover it's the first book actually written by Erlbruch himself. It's this that lends the story its particular humour and that makes it ring so true. Erlbruch's next book, published the following year, is just as witty and convincing.* Leonard *is the title of the book and the name of a little boy with a phobia about dogs. The character was modelled on Erlbruch's own son, Leo. In fact there were real-life counterparts for all the rest of the family, including Leonard's grandmother, who crawls around with a bone in her mouth. The point of the exercise? To take away Leonard's fear of dogs. The end-pages were painted by the real Leo. Wolf Erlbruch commented at the time: 'Leo kept drawing scary-looking dogs until he wasn't afraid of them any more.' That's one function of art. The 1995 continuation of the family saga* Mrs Meier the Bird *displays the same simple brilliance. Everything is present in equal measure – biographical background, the details of the artwork, the reference to art history and, most important of all, the story.*

This is where my favourite picture book comes in. In Night, *the very essence of every good illustration - the way in which the world of text is mirrored and transformed in pictures - becomes the theme and guiding principle of the book. It's the middle of the night and little Fons can't sleep, so he wakes his father and they walk together through the pitch-black city. And while the most amazing things are happening all around them, the father walks hand in hand with his son, dragging his feet, his eyes barely open, insisting that everyone's sleeping and that there's nothing to see. He doesn't notice that there's a fish pushing a strawberry in a pram, that the bridge is in fact the back of a dog, that a gorilla has lent his son a helping hand — he sees nothing at all! At the end of the book the father is tucked back up in bed, and, of course, there's nothing going on at night: 'It's just dark.' This wonderful little book could be read as an extended comment on the difference between children and adults.*

And that's one of Erlbruch's greatest strengths: he paints the child into the adult world and the adult into the world of children. The two worlds exist alongside one another, and neither has priority over the other. Children and adults smile across at each other with tenderness, affection and perhaps a little irritation. That's why it's so much better for adults and children to stand up straight and speak for themselves, father and son, or - as in In the Beginning - *God and man. That way everybody's happy and nobody loses out.*

Of course, there are also all the other books that Erlbruch has illustrated: his pictures for Gioconda Belli's The Butterfly Workshop, *his version of Goethe's* Das Hexeneinmaleins *and his superb edition of Karl Philipp Moritz's* Neues ABC-Buch. *These illustrations are worthy of a gallery wall - for art-lovers they're a delight.*

And yet it's the other books I find most moving. No fantasy adventures, no social problems and no heroes - just simple, quiet stories. About not being able to sleep at night, about grandpa dying, about wanting to have someone to hug, about taking care of the bird that can't fly. Or about getting up every day and having to create a bit more world. Just simple stories that become great books.

Konrad Heidkamp
Children's books editor of Die Zeit

Magus Lupus: a proposito del Mago Wolf Erlbruch

Le medaglie Hans Christian Andersen 2006 per la scrittura e l'illustrazione hanno avvicinato due artisti che, pur provenendo da parti diverse del mondo, occupano, per molti aspetti, lo stesso spazio mentale: Margaret Mahy, artista di talento della Nuova Zelanda, e Wolf Erlbruch, artista tedesco di collage, bizzarrie, e un catalogo riattualizzato di stili passati. Entrambi celebrano la meraviglia per il mondo come lo vivono i più piccoli: un dono di percezione che i più giovani hanno ma che gli adulti, spesso troppo pieni di sé, rifiutano in quanto fantastico, improbabile e puerile.

Mahy si rammarica del fatto che "siamo predisposti geneticamente a filtrare la meraviglia fuori dalla nostra vita, ad imparare a dare per scontate le cose straordinarie, in modo da non sprecare troppe energie nel sorprenderci per poter continuare a mangiare, accoppiarci, fare giardinaggio, dar da mangiare al gatto, lamentarci delle tasse, e così via." Wolf Erlbruch sarebbe certamente d'accordo. Infatti, sulla profondità della percezione dei bambini, sulla loro capacità di vedere cose alle quali i loro genitori restano o sono diventati insensibili, egli ha detto le stesse cose. "Nessun bambino è ignorante" ha scritto. "Questo è solo ciò che piace pensare agli adulti, per poter avere un vantaggio su di loro, mentre è esattamente il contrario: gli adulti vivono con una tale quantità di limitazioni che non riescono semplicemente a scandagliare la profondità intellettuale dei bambini." In tutta la sua opera, Erlbruch sembra determinato a dimostrare che nulla è banale, nulla è come gli adulti insistono che sia, nemmeno contare fino a dieci, nemmeno camminare lungo una strada buia in città, ma che tutto riecheggia di associazioni, fantasmi e possibilità miracolose.

Prendiamo il libro *La grande domanda*, pubblicato per la prima volta in Francia nel 2003 con il titolo *La grande question* e vincitore nel 2004 del BolognaRagazzi Award nella sezione fiction. La "grande domanda" non è altro che: Perché sono qui? Che occasione per i pedanti! Qualcuno potrebbe suggerire un confronto tra visione cristiana, buddista, esistenzialista e materialista del significato della vita! Erlbruch, invece, interroga un mucchio di persone, animali e persino oggetti inanimati presenti nella vita di un bambino, rivelando che ciascuno vede l'esistenza come un'estensione della propria vita. Questa splendida opera ci insegna che quel che conta sono le cose che danno un significato alla vita, che forniscono un contrasto umoristico alla serietà di certe persone, che portano l'amore nella nostra vita. È per questo che siamo qui. Ma visto che persino una tale affermazione potrebbe privare i bambini della loro voce, ci sono pagine bianche alla fine del libro dove ognuno può aggiungere le proprie risposte, che si evolvono con il passare degli anni. Assaporare i libri illustrati da Erlbruch è come ritrovarsi bambini di nuovo immersi nella misteriosa magia del mondo che ci circonda. Il fatto che tutto attorno a noi ci parli, sembra essere sottolineato dalla tecnica usata da Erlbruch. Nei suoi collage troviamo spesso ritagli di quotidiani o di libri contabili che (ci piaccia o no) ci parlano.

Contenuto e forma svolgono entrambi un ruolo altrettanto avvincente. Wolf Erlbruch è uno dei grandi innovatori e sperimentatori nell'arte dell'illustrazione. Usa abilmente una vasta gamma di registri artistici, è a suo agio nel citare e combinare stili artistici del XIX e del XX secolo, inventando – al tempo stesso – nuovi modi di raggiungere i bambini di tutte le età. Avvertiamo gli echi della tavolozza di colori e lo stile aspro della Germania di Weimar, delle figure e delle forme di Wilhelm Busch, gli straordinari collage di Max Ernst, tracce di Picasso, tocchi di Dalì, l'eccentricità di Bosch, e molto ancora. Eppure Erlbruch non è solo un semplice rimaneggiatore postmodernista di stili passati. Egli percorre strade completamente nuove, a volte semplici ed essenziali, altre volte intense ed intricate, restando sempre giocoso, ironico, filosofico, iconoclasta.

Iconoclasta? Ebbene sì. Renate Raecke, nel suo saggio per la candidatura di Erlbruch alla medaglia Hans Christian Andersen, ha osservato che i suoi personaggi *sono individualisti inimitabili, con le loro forme e contorni particolari, che non hanno nulla a che vedere con i soliti coniglietti, anatroccoli o caprette che si trovano negli altri libri per ragazzi e nei libri illustrati. Sono al di sopra di ogni tipo di carineria o banalizzazione. Non sono personaggi trattati con "l'ammorbidente" usato nei libri per ragazzi.*

Erlbruch non è affatto contrario alla grossolanità e al grottesco. Secondo Horst Künnemann, egli di fatto sfida costantemente "la tradizionale schizzinosità" e come egli stesso ha affermato, i ragazzi "hanno diritto ad illustrazioni contenenti una certa dose di crudezza." Così, mentre estende i limiti della pagina, Erlbruch estende anche i limiti di ciò che è accettabile. Forse la sua opera più brillante e profonda è quella che riguarda la sofferenza di una orchessa che ha una particolare predisposizione a mangiare bambini, *L'ogresse en pleurs*. Erlbruch amplia i limiti degli standard artistici e morali dei suoi giovani lettori (così come vengono intesi convenzionalmente) ma soprattutto amplia la loro immaginazione, nutrendo nei ragazzi quella stessa forza che stimola la sua arte. Quello che evoca è un mondo artistico, poetico e spesso magico, un mondo che segue leggi diverse da quelle della fisica.

Una sensibilità straordinaria per la storia, per la meraviglia e la bellezza, per quelle realtà che vanno al di là del rispecchiare in modo imperturbabile il fatto fisico, sono quindi qualità dell'infanzia che la letteratura per ragazzi dovrebbe nutrire, non cercare di sopraffare. Wolf Erlbruch è un mago al servizio di questa altissima missione.

Jeffrey Garrett
Presidente della giuria del Premio H. C. Andersen 2006

*Letter "P".
People at a dinner table
black dog*

Letter "S". Sick man with bloodbowl

Magus Lupus: About the Magician Wolf Erlbruch

The 2006 Hans Christian Andersen medals for writing and illustration brought two artists together who come from opposite corners of the world, yet in many ways occupy the same mental space: the gifted New Zealand artist Margaret Mahy and Wolf Erlbruch, the German artist of collage, grotesquerie, and a revivified catalog of past styles. Both of them celebrate the wonder of the world as young people experience it—a gift of perception which the young have but which their elders so often smugly reject as fantastic, implausible, and immature.

Mahy has lamented that 'we are biologically engineered to have the wonder filtered out of our lives, to learn to take astonishing things for granted so that we don't waste too much energy on being surprised but get on with the eating and mating, gardening, feeding cats, complaining about taxes, and so on'.

Wolf Erlbruch would surely agree. In fact, on the profundity of children's perception, on their ability to see things their parents remain blind to or have become blind to, he has said these things himself. 'No child is ignorant', he has written. 'That's only what adults like to think. They like to have the edge on them. But it's just the other way around. Grownups live with so many restrictions. They just can't fathom the intellectual depth of children'. In his entire oeuvre, Erlbruch seems determined to show that nothing is banal, nothing is as the grownups insist that it is—not even counting to ten, not even walking through a dark city street—but that everything resonates with associations, ghosts, and miraculous possibilities.

Let us consider his work The Big Question, *first published in France in 2003 as* La grande question *and the winner of the Bologna Ragazzi Award in the fiction section, in 2004. The 'big question' is no less than: Why am I here? What an opportunity for pedants this topic would offer! Let us compare (one of them might say) the Christian, Buddhist, existentialist, and materialist views of the meaning of life! But instead, Erlbruch queries a host of people, animals, and even inanimate objects in a child's life, revealing that each sees existence as an extension of their own lives. What matters, this beautiful book teaches us, are the things that give life meaning, that provide a humorous contrast to some people's seriousness, that bring love into our lives. That is why we are here. But since even that assertion could be depriving a child of her own voice, there are blank pages at the end of the book where a child can add her own evolving answers as she grows up.*

Experiencing Erlbruch's picture books is to be immersed again, as a child, in the numinosity of the world around us. That everything around us speaks to us seems underscored by Erlbruch's technique. His collages frequently incorporate scraps of newspapers or ledger sheets which, whether we want them to or not, speak to us.

Content and form play equally compelling roles and in both Wolf Erlbruch is one of the great innovators and

Letter "L". Girl with hat / lamb white line on black

experimenters of the illustrator's art. He masters an array of artistic registers, is as at home citing and combining artistic styles of the 19th and 20th centuries as he is inventing new ways to reach out to children of all ages. We sense echoes of the color palette and grainy style of Weimar Germany, of the shapes and forms of Wilhelm Busch, of Max Ernst's extraordinary collages, hints of Picasso, dashes of Dali, the eccentricities of Bosch, and much more. And yet Erlbruch is not a mere postmodernist remixer of the old. He goes entirely new ways. Sometimes simple and elemental, at other times dense and intricate, he is always playful, humorous, philosophical, iconoclastic.

Iconoclastic? Yes, indeed. Renate Raecke observed in her nomination essay for the Hans Christian Andersen Medal that 'Erlbruch's characters are inimitable individualists with their own unique forms and contours that have nothing at all to do with the usual bunnies, duckies, or wee billy goats found in other children's and picture books. They are above any type of cutesiness or trivialization. They have not been treated with a 'fabric softener' for children's books'.

Erlbruch is not at all averse to crassness and the grotesque. To quote Horst Künnemann, Erlbruch in fact consistently challenges 'traditional squeamishness'. Or as Erlbruch himself said, children 'are entitled to illustrations that have a certain crudeness'. And so, just as he stretches the limits of the page, Erlbruch also often stretches the limits of acceptable content. Consider that perhaps his most brilliant and profound work is about the suffering of an ogress who has a penchant for eating young children, L'ogresse en pleurs (The Sobbing Ogress, 1996).

Erlbruch stretches the limits of artistic and (conventionally understood) moral standards of his young readers, but above all he stretches their imaginations, nurturing that same power in children that propels his own art. It is an artistic, poetic, and often magical world which he conjures up, one that follows different laws than those of physics.

A powerful sense of story and of wonder and of beauty, of realities that go beyond the stolid mirroring of physical fact, are therefore qualities of childhood that children's literature should be nurturing, not seeking to overcome. Wolf Erlbruch is a magician in the service of this high calling.

Jeffrey Garrett
President of the 2006 H. C. Andersen Award Jury

LA MOSTRA DEGLI ILLUSTRATORI

La Mostra degli Illustratori, organizzata dalla Fiera del Libro per Ragazzi di Bologna, è uno dei più grandi e prestigiosi concorsi internazionali dedicati interamente alle illustrazioni di libri per bambini e ragazzi. Nata nel 1967, la Mostra giunge quest'anno alla quarantunesima edizione senza interruzione. Hanno partecipato alla selezione oltre 2600 illustratori da circa 60 paesi: tra questi, una giuria internazionale ha selezionato 85 artisti. Se da un lato la Mostra degli Illustratori ha l'obiettivo di approfondire le possibilità espressive dell'illustrazione dei libri per l'infanzia, dall'altro essa costituisce una occasione unica per gli illustratori di presentare le loro opere nell'ambito del mercato editoriale internazionale, e per gli editori di scoprire nuovi talenti. In questo modo, la Fiera del Libro per Ragazzi - il più importante appuntamento mondiale per il settore - diventa uno dei punti di incontro dove vengono discussi in modo concreto nuovi progetti di libri e, nello stesso tempo, la Mostra si offre come tappa di passaggio e trampolino di lancio per farsi conoscere nel mondo editoriale. Una delle caratteristiche fondamentali di questa Mostra sta nel fatto che la partecipazione è aperta a tutti gli illustratori, sia esordienti sia già pubblicati. Questo produce un interessantissimo mix, in cui opere di artisti affermati si alternano a lavori di giovani studenti, offrendo numerosi spunti per la previsione delle nuove tendenze editoriali e dell'illustrazione nel mondo.

IL CAFFE' DEGLI ILLUSTRATORI

Durante la Fiera del Libro per Ragazzi, nella stessa area dedicata alla Mostra degli Illustratori (che si trova proprio all'ingresso della Fiera), viene realizzata una arena dedicata agli incontri, ai dibattiti e ai workshop sull'illustrazione e sull'editoria per l'infanzia. Qui si svolge anche la cerimonia di premiazione della Mostra degli Illustratori, un momento in cui gli illustratori selezionati di tutto il mondo possono incontrarsi e scambiarsi informazioni. Si svolge nello stesso spazio anche il ben noto incontro fra i membri della giuria e gli illustratori, in cui vengono presentati i criteri seguiti dalla commissione nelle sue scelte.
E' molto atteso anche l'incontro con l'autore della copertina dell'Annual, alternativamente il vincitore del Grand Prix della Biennale di Illustrazione di Bratislava (BIB) e del Premio Andersen; in questa occasione spesso gli artisti improvvisano performance e conversano direttamente con gli aspiranti autori di libri per l'infanzia.
Nel 2006, il Caffè degli Illustratori ha riservato un ampio spazio a uno dei più noti esponenti dell'illustrazione italiana, Roberto Innocenti, a cui è stato dedicato una retrospettiva nel palazzo comunale di Bologna durante la manifestazione.

LA MOSTRA DEGLI ILLUSTRATORI NEL MONDO

Dopo i quattro giorni della Fiera del Libro per Ragazzi, la Mostra degli Illustratori intraprende il suo viaggio nel mondo grazie alla collaborazione con JBBY (Japanese Board on Books for Young People - sezione giapponese di IBBY). La Mostra è tradizionalmente ospitata in quattro musei d'arte del Giappone e, da più di venticinque anni, è diventata un appuntamento molto rinomato in tutto il paese. La Mostra degli Illustratori ha stimolato in questi anni il pubblico giapponese a guardare le illustrazioni come opere d'arte. E' considerata un evento grazie al quale i bambini possono avere un primo approccio con l'arte. In molti musei, le illustrazioni sono appese ad un'altezza adatta alla visione del pubblico più giovane e le didascalie sono scritte in un linguaggio molto facile. Durante la Mostra, nei musei si svolgono workshop per illustratori, per le scuole e per le famiglie.
I workhop per illustratori, che si tengono ogni anno all'Itabashi Art Museum durante l'esposizione della Mostra, hanno stimolato la nascita di vari progetti di libri, alcuni dei quali sono stati pubblicati. Inoltre, grazie alle attività promozionali svolte nei musei, la partecipazione di illustratori giapponesi alla Mostra di Bologna continua a crescere ogni anno. La Mostra degli Illustratori è diventata un punto d'incontro non solo per chi lavora nell'ambiente e per chi ama l'illustrazione, ma anche per grafici, artisti, insegnanti e famiglie, perché è riconosciuta come un evento artistico che permette di ammirare illustrazioni da prospettive sempre nuove.
Nell'anno 2006, la Mostra degli Illustratori in Giappone ha avuto l'onore di ricevere la visita di Sua Altezza l'Imperatrice Michiko, nota per il suo profondo interesse per i libri per bambini. Durante la visita all'Itabashi Art Museum, Sua Altezza ha osservato con entusiasmo ogni opera, con l'assistenza di giovani artisti che le hanno illustrato le storie e le tecniche usate.
Nel dicembre 2007, la Mostra partirà dal Giappone verso la Corea, per una prestigiosa tappa alla

---

L'ITINERARIO INTERNAZIONALE DELLA MOSTRA 2007/2008

Itabashi Art Museum
Tokyo, Giappone
4 luglio - 19 agosto 2007

Otani Memorial Art Museum
Nishinomiya, Giappone
25 agosto - 30 settembre 2007

Kawara Museum
Takahama, Giappone
6 ottobre - 4 novembre 2007

Ishikawa Nanao Art Museum
Nanao, Giappone
10 novembre - 9 dicembre 2007

Neverland Picture Book Gallery
Paju (Seoul), Corea
28 dicembre 2007 - 10 febbraio 2008

THE ILLUSTRATORS EXHIBITION

The Illustrators Exhibition, organized by the Bologna Children's Book Fair, is one of the largest and the most prestigious international competitions devoted entirely to books for children and teenagers.
Since the first edition on 1967, the exhibition has been held for forty one years without interruption. A total of more than 2,600 illustrators from some 60 countries took part in this year's selection, and 85 of them were selected by an international jury. The Illustrators Exhibition has the aim of exploring the expressive potential of children's book illustration while being a unique opportunity for illustrators to present their works to the international publishing market and for the publishers to discover new talents. This way the Bologna Children's Book Fair – the most important event of its kind in the world – becomes a forum for concrete discussion of new projects for books.
One of the important factors of this exhibition is the fact that partecipation is open to all illustrators, whether they have already published their works or are just at the beginning of their careers. This creates an interesting mix in which the works of established artists alternate with those of young people and students, offering a vast opportunity to predict new trends in publishing and of the illustration worldwide.

THE ILLUSTRATORS CAFE'

During the Bologna Children's Book Fair, the space dedicated to the Illustrators Exhibition will include an arena for meetings, debates, workshops on illustration and children's publishing. This will also be the venue for the Illustrators Exhibition award ceremony, where selected illustrators from all over the world meet and exchange information.
During the meeting between members of the jury and the illustrators, one of the main highlights of the Illustrators Café, the jury outline the criteria they have followed in making their selections for the Illustrators Exhibition. Another popular event is the meeting with the creator of the Annual cover, alternated annually by the Grand Prix winner at the Biennal of Illustrations in Bratislava (BIB) and the Andersen Award winner.
In 2006, the Café focused on Roberto Innocenti, one of the leading artists in Italian book illustration. A special exhibit of his works covering the whole of his career was held in the town hall during the Bologna Children's Book Fair.

THE ILLUSTRATORS EXHIBITION WORLDWIDE

After the four days of the Bologna Children's Book Fair, the Illustrators Exhibition will be embarking on its worldwide trip organized in cooperation with JBBY (Japanese Board on Books for Young People - Japanese section of IBBY).
The exhibition is traditionally held in four different Japanese art museums. It has been organised for more than twenty-five years and is famous all over the country. The Illustrators Exhibition has encouraged the Japanese public to look at illustrations as works of art. Furthermore, it is seen as an exhibition where children can approach art for the first time. In many of the museums, the illustrations are hung at a suitable height for children and the captions are written in simple language. During the Exhibition, the museums hold workshops for illustrators, schools and families.
The workshops for illustrators, held every year in the Itabashi Art Museum during the Illustrators Exhibition, have resulted in a number of book projects, some of which have been published. Thanks to the promotional activities carried out by the museums, Japanese participation in the Bologna Illustrators Exhibition is increasing steadily every year. The Illustrators Exhibition has become a meeting point not only for professionals and enthusiasts, but also for graphic designers, artists, teachers and families. It is seen as an artistic event where illustrations can be admired from a fresh perspective every year.
In 2006, the Illustratrors Exhibition in Japan was visited by Her Majesty Empress Michiko, known for her profound interest in children's books. During the visit to the Itabashi Art Museum, Her Majesty observed each illustration with great enthusiasm with the assistance of young artists who explained the stories represented and the techniques used.
In December 2007, after Japan, the Exhibition will be making its first prestigious visit to Korea to the Seoul Neverland Picture Book Gallery.

ITABASHI ART MUSEUM
Entrance of the Itabashi Art Museum

NISHINOMIYA – Otani Memorial Art Exhibition

NANAO - Ishikawa Nanao Art Museum Exhibition

YOKKAICHI - Municipal Museum Entrance

NAGASHIMA Art Museum
They are having a picture book read

THE 2007/2008 EXHIBITION INTERNATIONAL ITINERARY

Itabashi Art Museum
Tokyo, Japan
4 July - 19 August 2007

Otani Memorial Art Museum
Nishinomiya, Japan
25 August - 30 September 2007

Kawara Museum
Takahama, Japan
6 October - 4 November 2007

Ishikawa Nanao Art Museum
Nanao, Japan
10 November - 9 December 2007

Neverland Picture Book Gallery
Paju (Seoul), Korea
28 December 2007 - 10 February 2008

Membri della Commissione Internazionale di Selezione 2007

Members of the 2007 International Selection Committee

Jeffrey Garrett
Northwestern University
Chicago, USA

Katsumi Komagata
Artist and publisher
Tokyo, Japan

Fausta Orecchio
Edizioni Orecchio Acerbo
Rome, Italy

Lisbeth Zwerger
Artist
Vienna, Austria

JEFFREY GARRETT nasce nel 1949 ad Evanston, città universitaria a nord di Chicago dove entrambi i genitori hanno studiato presso la Northwestern University. Dopo gli studi, fa il servizio di leva a Francoforte dove riceve una formazione di interprete per la lingua tedesca e al termine frequenta l'Università di Monaco dove si laurea in Linguistica e Storia Europea. Prosegue poi gli studi all'Università californiana di Berkeley dove viene nominato Regents Scholar. Oggi ricopre il ruolo di bibliotecario alla Northwestern dove è responsabile degli acquisti dei libri gestendo un bilancio annuale di circa nove milioni di dollari. Tuttavia negli ultimi 25 anni, oltre all'attività di bibliotecario, si dedica allo studio della letteratura infantile, un interesse nato quando faceva il traduttore e l'interprete presso la Biblioteca Internazionale per Ragazzi all'inizio degli anni Ottanta. Nell'83 diventa capo della sezione inglese della stessa e nell'85 visita per la prima volta la Fiera del Libro per Ragazzi. Nei cinque anni che vi trascorre, organizza diverse mostre, grandi e piccole, su temi che spaziano dalla lingua celtica nei libri per ragazzi agli illustratori internazionali di "Alice nel Paese delle Meraviglie". Nel 1990, la sezione americana dell'IBBY fa il suo nome per la Giuria del Premio Hans Christian Andersen di cui farà parte nel 1992 a Basilea e nel 1994 a Copenhagen. Nello stesso periodo, viene nominato coeditore assieme a Lucia Binder della rivista internazionale dell'IBBY Bookbird che rinnova completamente. Torna nella Giuria del premio Andersen che presiede nel 2004 e nel 2006. Ha scritto molto sull'illustrazione internazionale per ragazzi anche con un saggio sugli illustratori di Hans Christian Andersen per "Andersen torna a casa: l'Esposizione del Bicentenario in Sala Borsa", Bologna, 2005. Assieme ai colleghi della Northwestern, nel 2000, ha portato a Chicago la Mostra degli Illustratori di Bologna.

Non è un'iperbole dire che la Mostra degli Illustratori di Bologna è l'evento più democratico di tutto il panorama dell'editoria per ragazzi. Qualsiasi artista al mondo che abbia il desiderio e l'ispirazione (e che si possa permettere le spese postali) può concorrere per avere un proprio spazio in questa mostra, che non si tiene in un padiglione lontano del quartiere fieristico, già a metà strada per Ferrara, ma proprio vicino all'ingresso principale, nel cuore della fiera. Le opere scelte dalla giuria vengono viste da centinaia di migliaia di persone: altri artisti, curatori, editori, dalla stampa, per non citare le decine di migliaia di visitatori durante il tour in Asia orientale. Sono inoltre riprodotte con cura nel catalogo, raggiungendo così indirettamente altre migliaia di persone. Riuscire a partecipare a questa mostra è una sfida, la stessa per ciascun concorrente, e può essere così riassunta: "Artista! (se è così che ti definisci!) Cosa sai dire, che storia sai raccontare, come sai presentare nel modo più efficace ed eloquente te stesso, le tue abilità e il tuo messaggio con appena cinque immagini in sequenza?"
Credo che, anche per gli artisti il cui lavoro alla fine non viene accettato, partecipare alla

JEFFREY GARRETT was born in 1949 in Evanston, a college town north of Chicago, where his parents were both students at Northwestern University. After school he served in the U.S. Army in Frankfurt, where he was trained as an interpreter for German. Once his military service was completed, he attended the University of Munich, graduating with honors in Linguistics and European History, and continued his education at the University of California at Berkeley, where he was named a Regents Scholar. Today he is the assistant university librarian at the same university his parents attended - Northwestern - with responsibility for an annual acquisitions budget of about nine million dollars. In addition to his vocation as a professional librarian, his chief avocation over the last 25 years has been children's literature studies. This interest began when he served as a translator and interpreter for the International Youth Library in the early 1980s. He became head of the IYL's English Language Section in 1983, just when it moved from its old home in the Kaulbachstrasse to Schloss Blutenburg on the outskirts of Munich. He attended the Bologna Children's Book Fair for the first time in 1985. During his five years at the IYL, he organized exhibits large and small on topics ranging from Celtic-language children's books to international illustrators of Alice in Wonderland. In 1990 he was nominated by the U.S. IBBY Section to serve on IBBY's Hans Christian Andersen Award Jury, which he served on in 1992 in Basel and in 1994 in Copenhagen. At about the same time, he was appointed co-editor, with Lucia Binder, of IBBY's international magazine Bookbird, which he completely redesigned. He returned to the Andersen Jury as its president in 2004 and again in 2006. He has written extensively on international children's book illustration, including an essay on illustrators of Hans Christian Andersen for the 2005 Bologna publication, 'Andersen torna a casa: l'Esposizione del Bicentenario in Sala Borsa". With colleagues at Northwestern, he also brought the entire Bologna Illustrators Exhibit to Chicago in 2000.

It is not hyperbole to say that the Illustrators Exhibit in Bologna is the most democratic event in the whole world of children's publishing. Any artist in the world who has the will and the inspiration - and can afford the postage - can compete for a spot in this show. And it's located not in some distant hall of the fairgrounds already halfway to Ferrara, but right near the main entrance, at the heart of the fair. The works chosen by the jury are seen by hundreds of thousands of people: by other artists, by editors, publishers, and the press, not mention by the scores of thousands of visitors during the East Asian tour. They are also reproduced lovingly in the catalog, reaching then even more thousands of people indirectly. The challenge to get into this exhibit is the same for each competitor and can be summarized thus: Artist! (If that's what you call yourself!) What can you say, what story can you tell, how can you most effectively and eloquently present yourself and your skill and your message in just five successive images?

competizione di Bologna sia un ottimo esercizio. Non ci sono cartelline sfavillanti che diano vantaggio allo sfrontato che si auto-promuove con i propri mezzi. I giurati non vedono la foto dell'artista. Sul modulo di partecipazione non c'è spazio per una lettera di presentazione (in effetti, c'è a malapena spazio sufficiente per le didascalie). C'è solo l'ordine delle immagini, numerate da uno a cinque, il che significa che c'è per lo meno un invito a raccontare una storia, oppure no. Il messaggio a chi presenta le proprie opere a Bologna è chiaro: la vostra arte deve saper parlare da sola. Il grande illustratore di libri uruguaiano Antonio Fiasconi, dieci o quindici anni fa, durante una sua mostra presso la Biblioteca del Congresso, commentava che, oggi, si trovano illustrazioni serie solo nei libri per ragazzi. Per una qualche oscura ragione, nella grande divisione del lavoro che caratterizza i nostri tempi, ai ragazzi, viene affidata la responsabilità di scegliere i migliori illustratori di libri. Se loro ti accettano, puoi diventare ricco e famoso a livello internazionale. A Bologna mi sono sentito il fautore ed il rappresentante di questi ragazzi. A loro cosa piacerà di più? A cosa faranno il dono della loro attenzione, delle loro risate, della loro tristezza? Quali artisti vorranno riguardarsi e richiederanno sempre ai genitori? Oppure, domanda altrettanto importante, quali artisti incontreranno una sola volta senza rivederli mai più, custodendone però nel cuore un ricordo indelebile?
È così che ho vissuto il mio lavoro a Bologna, immaginando di sedermi ad un tavolo con un artista e un ragazzo, presentarli l'uno all'altro, quindi fare un passo indietro e vedere cosa succedeva.

Even for artists whose work is ultimately not accepted, I believe that entering the Bologna competition is an excellent exercise. There is no glitzy dossier, which gives an advantage to the shameless self-promoter of independent means. The jurors don't see photos of the artist. On the entry form there is no room for a letter of introduction - in fact, there is barely enough room for captions. There is only the order of the images, 'one' through 'five," meaning there is at least an invitation to tell a story - or not. The message to those who submit their art to Bologna is clear: your art must speak for itself. The great Uruguayan book illustrator Antonio Frasconi commented during an exhibit of his works at the Library of Congress ten or fifteen years ago that today, serious book illustration really only takes place in books for children. In the great division of labor within our modern world, children, for whatever obscure reason, have been assigned responsibility for choosing the world's most talented book artists. If children accept you, you can become wealthy and internationally famous.
In Bologna, I felt myself to be the advocate and representative of these children. What will they like best? What will they be most likely to reward with the gift of their attention, their laughter, their consternation? Which artists would they be most likely to return to, to ask their parents to show them again and again? Or just as potentially important: which artists they meet just once and do not return to might nonetheless remain permanently in their memories?
That was my job in Bologna, as I saw it. To sit at a table with an artist and a child. To introduce them to one another. And then to lean back and to see what happens.

KATSUMI KOMAGATA è nato in Giappone nel 1953 e si trasferisce negli Stati Uniti nel 1977 dove lavora come graphic designer, in particolare alla CBS Inc. nella sede di New York. Nel 1983, torna in Giappone e nel 1986 fonda la One Stroke. Nel 1992, pubblica per Kaiseisha 10 serie di carte "Little Eyes" ed altri libri tra i quali "Blue to Blue", "I'm Gonna be Born", "Tears", "Found it" per la One Stroke. Realizza libri per non-vedenti per il Centro Pompidou, "Les trois ourses", "Les doigts qui rêvent", e negli ultimi anni per la One Stroke. Il percorso creativo di Komagata si è sviluppato su più fronti, in special modo attraverso i libri e i giocattoli educativi che gli hanno valso importanti riconoscimenti a livello internazionale come la Menzione Speciale del BolognaAward della Fiera del Libro per Ragazzi. Le sue mostre e i suoi workshop, finalizzati allo scambio comunicativo tra generazioni, vengono organizzati in luoghi con forti legami con le comunità come le scuole, le biblioteche, le ludoteche, i musei, ecc., in Giappone e in altri paesi quali la Francia, l'Italia, la Svizzera, il Messico, la Nuova Caledonia, il Portogallo e la Corea.

KATSUMI KOMAGATA was born in Japan in 1953. In 1977 he moved to the US, where he worked as a graphic designer, most notably at CBS Inc. in New York. In 1983 he returned to Japan and in 1986 set up One Stroke. In 1992 he released 10 series of 'Little Eyes' card storybooks for Kaiseisha and later published various storybooks such as 'Blue to Blue', 'I'm Gonna be Born', 'Tears' and 'Found it' for One Stroke. In recent years he has created books for blind people for the Centre Pompidou, 'Les trois ourses', 'Les doigts qui rêvent' and One Stroke. His creative work has expanded to include fiction storybooks, toys for intellectual education, etc., and has won him globally renowned awards such as the Special Mention Award at the Bologna Children's Book Fair. His exhibitions and workshops are held both in Japan and in other countries worldwide including France, Italy, Switzerland, Mexico, New Caledonia, Portugal and Korea. His workshops are held at locations with strong ties to the community such as schools, libraries, children's centres, museums, etc., and have become forums for communication between different generations.

Nel momento in cui sono entrato nella sala, sono rimasto sbalordito dalla quantità delle opere. Un gran numero di illustrazioni erano stese sui tavoli lasciando ben poco spazio tra l'una e l'altra. Per iniziare, ho deciso di considerare tutte le opere alla pari senza alcun preconcetto. Ho cercato di selezionare quelle illustrazioni che sentivo promettenti anche se potevano essere ancora tecnicamente immature o mancanti di forza espressiva. Poi, tra quelle opere che mi hanno catturato fin dall'inizio, ho scelto quelle che erano leggibili come racconto. La mia priorità assoluta era "il contatto visuale". In generale, la mia impressione è stata che, nonostante la strutturazione in cinque scene, le opere mancassero di espressività e fossero "piatte" (monotone). C'erano poche sorprese quando giravi la pagina, alle composizioni mancava il senso di ritmo, c'erano pochi contrasti , per esempio, tra forte-grande e silenzioso-piccolo. Molte delle opere in effetti mantenevano lo stesso volume di espressività in tutte le cinque scene. Dal secondo giorno, abbiamo esaminato le illustrazioni insieme, controllando ogni singola illustrazione e rovesciando le opere da scartare. La frase "girale" si sentiva molto spesso. Era chiaro che molte illustrazioni erano difficilmente riproducibili. Soprattutto quelle con foglie d'oro o piume di uccelli. L'utilizzo di questi elementi spesso non era riuscito e quindi non venivano selezionate.

C'era un set di illustrazioni che mi interessava. Un verde scuro era steso su tutta la pagina in cui si vedevano dei piccoli animali, puntini e linee. I colori erano fosforescenti… era ovvio che i colori sarebbero stati difficili da riprodurre in stampa. Ciò nonostante, le ho selezionate senza esitazione. Era perché svelavano uno spirito di "sfida". Quando stai cercando di esprimere qualcosa attraverso la stampa, in un certo senso stai "mirando a qualcosa in più" rispetto all'originale. Le tecniche di stampa che servono per realizzare queste intenzioni stanno migliorando sempre di più. Io vorrei che i giovani illustratori comprendessero cos'è la stampa, e che cercassero di creare qualcosa di migliore con quella conoscenza. In altre parole, è quel limite che ha la stampa che rende possibile la creazione di opere più interessanti. Ora ci sono tanti tipi di tecniche di processi di stampa oltre a quella offset a quattro colori, come la stampa con inchiostro speciale fluorescente, stampa a rilievo, stampa a caldo, ecc., ma questi sistemi alzano i costi di produzione. Vorrei vedere gli illustratori "aspirare a qualcosa in più" per superare queste difficoltà. Essere un membro della giuria mi ha messo in contatto con una grande quantità di energia creativa. Potete immaginare che anche la mia volontà creativa era rinnovata. Forse stavo dimenticando la parola "sfida". L'evoluzione delle forme di vita è chiamata differenziazione o diversità, mentre "l'uniformità" è considerata "degenerazione". Le varie culture, gli ambienti, le razze e i valori visti in queste opere raccolte sopra un unico palcoscenico costituivano la "diversità" stessa. Molto positiva anche la libertà di selezionare un numero aperto di artisti, senza considerare la selezione come una competizione a premi. Dopo i tre giorni di selezione, sono stati scelti un totale di ottantacinque artisti tra fiction e non-fiction. Uno

The moment I entered the hall, I was astounded by the quantity of works. An infinite number of illustrations were laid out upon the tables with almost no space in-between. To start with, I decided to look at all the works as equals without any preconceptions. I tried to sort out those illustrations that I felt were promising, even though they might still be technically immature or lacking in expressive strength. Then, from those works that captivated me at the beginning, I picked out those that were readable as a story. My highest priority was 'visual contact'. My general impression was that even though the works were structured with five scenes, they were rather limited in expression and were 'flat' (monotonous). There were few surprises when you turned the page, very little rhythm was felt in the compositions, few changes in contrast between strong and big or silent and small. Many of the works in fact maintained the same level of expressiveness throughout the five scenes. From the second day, we examined the works together. We checked each of the works and turned over the illustrations that were to be eliminated. The phrase 'turn it over' was heard very often. It was clear that many of the works would be hard to reproduce in print. Especially those with gold leaves or bird feathers. Use of these elements was often unsuccessful and as a result the works did not get selected.

There was one set of illustrations that interested me. Dark green was spread on the whole page, and in it you could see little animals, dots and lines. The colours were fluorescent… it was obvious that the colours would be difficult to reproduce in print. Nevertheless, I went ahead and selected them. It was because of the spirit of 'challenge' that they revealed.

When you are trying to express something in the printed form, in a certain sense you 'aim at something higher' than the original. Printing techniques that realize those intentions are being improved. I would like young illustrators to understand what printing is and to try to use that knowledge to make something even better. In other words, it is the limitation of printing that makes it possible to create more interesting works. Now there are many kinds of processing techniques besides four-colour process offset, such as special colour printing with fluorescent ink, embossing, hot stamping, etc., but these raise production costs. I would like to see illustrators 'aim at something higher' so as to overcome these difficulties.

Being a jury member allowed me to come into contact with an enormous amount of creative energy. Needless to say, my will to create was also renewed. Maybe I was beginning to forget the word 'challenge'. Evolution of life forms is referred to as 'differentiation' or 'diversity', while 'uniformity' is considered 'degeneration'. The many cultures, backgrounds, races and values seen in the works gathered together onto a single stage truly represented 'diversity'. Other selection criteria such as 'liberty to choose as many artists as you like', without considering the selection as a competition with winners was also very nice. After a three-day judging process, a total of eighty-five artists from the fiction and non-fiction sections were selected. One of the judges unfortunately could not

dei membri della giuria purtroppo non ha potuto partecipare per ragioni di salute. Ciò nonostante, la selezione eseguita da noi quattro, ognuno con il proprio punto di vista, ha prodotto una scelta ricca e varia. Spero tanto che possiate venire alla Mostra per sentire l'energia creativa. Sentirete sicuramente quella pacca d'incoraggiamento sulla spalla grazie a quella energia chiamata spirito di "sfida".

participate due to health problems. Nevertheless, the selection made by the four of us, each with our own different standpoints, has achieved richness and variety. I hope that you will be able to come to the exhibition to experience the creative energy. I'm sure you'll feel that slap of encouragement on your back called the 'spirit of challenge'.

FAUSTA ORECCHIO è nata a Roma nel 1957. Avrebbe voluto essere una matematica o una musicista, ma è diventata grafica per punizione. A sedici anni, infatti, una sospensione scolastica le impedisce di proseguire gli studi e comincia così a lavorare allo Studio Giulio Italiani, dove apprende gli elementi basilari del graphic design. In seguito frequenta il corso di disegno del nudo all'Accademia di Belle Arti di Roma. Negli anni '80, abbandona definitivamente la musica per dedicarsi interamente alla grafica, che da punizione diventa finalmente passione. Nell'89 entra in contatto col gruppo di fumettisti "Valvoline". Lì comincia la collaborazione e l'amicizia con alcuni illustratori fra cui Lorenzo Mattotti, Igort, Francesca Ghermandi, Gabriella Giandelli, Stefano Ricci e molti altri. Sarà proprio questa collaborazione che di lì in poi segnerà fortemente il suo lavoro grafico.
Fra il '94 e il 2000 lavora particolarmente nel campo editoriale ridisegnando la linea grafica di importanti case editrici italiane. Nel 1997 ottiene il Premio Matita d'oro per il Graphic Design e, nel 2001, la Segnalazione d'onore nel concorso Compasso d'oro per il lavoro svolto per le riviste *Hands off Cain* e *Lo Straniero*.
Nel dicembre 2001 fonda la casa editrice Orecchio Acerbo il cui catalogo conta oggi oltre cinquanta titoli e che - nonostante i numerosi riconoscimenti per il suo impegno nel rinnovamento dell'editoria per ragazzi in Italia - giorno dopo giorno dilapida inesorabilmente le risorse accumulate in molti duri anni di lavoro grafico.
Malgrado i suoi numerosi e sempre strazianti traslochi - oltre 35 - continua a vivere a Roma e non ha ancora abbandonato l'idea che prima o poi diventerà una grande matematica.

FAUSTA ORECCHIO was born in Rome in 1957. She would have liked to have been a mathematician or a musician, but she became a graphic designer as a form of punishment. At the age of sixteen, she was suspended from school. Being unable to continue her studies, she began working at Studio Giulio Italiani, where she learned the basics of graphic design. She subsequently attended the nude drawing course at the Accademia di Belle Arti in Rome. In the 1980s she abandoned music to devote herself entirely to graphic design, which instead of a punishment had at last become a passion. In 1989 she came into contact with the 'Valvoline' group of comic-strip artists. It was there that she began her collaboration and friendship with illustrators Lorenzo Mattotti, Igort, Francesca Ghermandi, Gabriella Giandelli, Stefano Ricci and many more. This collaboration would strongly influence her design work in subsequent years. Between 1994 and 2000 she principally worked in the field of publishing, restyling the graphic images of leading Italian publishers. In 1997 she won the Matita d'oro (Golden Pencil) Award for Graphic Design and in 2001 an honourable mention in the Compasso d'oro (Golden compass) competition for her work for the magazines Hands off Cain and Lo Straniero. In December 2001 she founded the publishing house Orecchio Acerbo. It has a catalogue of more than fifty titles and, in spite of receiving numerous tributes for its efforts in modernising children's publishing in Italy, inexorably dissipates the resources Fausta has accumulated in many years of hard work as a graphic designer. In spite of her numerous and invariably traumatic moves – more than 35 to date – she continues to live in Rome and has not yet given up the idea that sooner or later she will become a great mathematician.

Come ogni giurato che si rispetti, comincio da un giuramento: giuro che non farò mai più il giurato. E spero che questo renderà più clementi dei miei – e più giudiziosi – i vostri giudizi sulla giuria, sui giurati, sul giudicare.
E poi un ringraziamento agli amici con cui ho condiviso questo compito: l'inflessibile e simpaticissima Lisbeth, il silenzioso e misterioso Katsumi, e Jeff, il poeta, cui dobbiamo le scelte più innovative di questa edizione della Mostra Illustratori. Ciascuno di loro mi ha fatto vedere le immagini da un altro punto di vista, con altri occhi. E, infine, voglio ringraziare chi ci ha ospitato in una Bologna davvero generosissima.

*Like any self-respecting jury member, I shall begin by swearing an oath: I swear that I shall never again be a member of a jury. I hope that this will make your judgements of the jury, the jury members and the very act of judging more clement and judicious than my own.
I would also like to thank the people I have shared this task with: the inflexible but most likeable Lisbeth, the silent and mysterious Katsumi, and Jeff the poet, to whom we owe the most innovative choices of this edition of the Illustrators Exhibition. Each of them made me look at images from*

Difficile descrivere quello che ho provato quando si sono aperte le porte del padiglione 18. Quindicimila disegni nudi in una sovraesposizione assoluta. Una quantità di lavoro enorme. La fatica, la speranza, la fragilità. La nostra responsabilità, la mia inadeguatezza, la mia parzialità. Ecco, in un attimo ho capito che non avrei potuto fare altro che essere, assolutamente, parziale. Non c'era, non c'è, alcuna possibilità di giudizio, ma solo una scelta, la mia, quella degli altri componenti della giuria. Ciascuno con la propria e diversa visione. Visioni lontane, ma - così mi è parso - un analogo approccio: il rispetto, e l'attenzione, per tutto quel lavoro, la noia per il decorativo, per gli esercizi di stile, la consapevolezza che quello dell'illustratore è un lavoro difficilissimo. Occorre esercizio, umiltà, capacità di confronto, flessibilità. Bisogna saper guardare, dentro e oltre sé stessi, saper raccontare. Quello che ho cercato, fra migliaia di illustrazioni, è stata l'intelligenza: quella narrativa, quella estetica. E poi l'autenticità. Ho provato a tenermi alla larga dal fasullo, dalle mode, dalle tendenze del momento. Ho provato a cercare l'autenticità nell'uso delle tecnologie, il computer usato per riprodurre non ciò che le mani sanno fare meglio, ma ciò che le mani non possono fare. Non "falsi" acrilici, ma "veri" Photoshop. Ho cercato il coraggio, quello della ricerca di forme o colori, e quello delle idee. Ho provato a distinguere l'abilità, la perizia tecnica, l'intelligenza delle mani. E, alla fine, ho ripercorso una per una le immagini che, fra mille, erano rimaste nella mia mente, anche se non tutte potrete vederle nella mostra di quest'anno: un ragazzo che uccide un cervo per rubargli il cuore / un "bogeyman" che muta i bambini in automi ubbidienti / una piccola gallina –leggerissima– che attende in panchina / un Testamento molto, molto speciale /un groviglio di carta tagliata / un gatto sopra un water / una macchina per asparagi giganteschi / delle oche molto stupide dai tratti veloci ed elegantissimi / una mucca che prende il tè in salotto / un mondo popolato da maiali terribilmente avidi / un Cappuccetto Rosso intrappolato in un videogame / le parole di una donna che come pesci scivolano via dalla sua bocca. E forse è questa l'immagine che più di ogni altra somiglia al mio stato d'animo: mi sono mancate, le parole. Mi è mancata quella miscela speciale di immagini e parole di cui sono fatti i libri illustrati. Come se, d'improvviso, da migliaia di immagini stese sui tavoli del padiglione 18 le parole fossero scivolate via come pesci per dirigersi altrove. Le ho cercate, le parole, nelle scarne didascalie poste dietro a ogni disegno. Ma qui, alla Mostra Illustratori, sono le immagini, sole, a dover raccontare le loro storie. E noi, saperle ascoltare. Non so se ne siamo stati capaci. Non so quanti –spero pochissimi– talenti siano rimasti fuori da questo catalogo e dalla mostra di quest'anno, ma sono certa che ve ne sono. Ma sono anche certa che le loro immagini troveranno altri e nuovi occhi, che sapranno guardarle, per ascoltare davvero la loro storia.

another perspective, with new eyes. Last but not least, I would like to thank our hosts in the wonderfully hospitable city of Bologna.
It is difficult for me to describe my sensations when the doors to hall 18 were opened to reveal fifteen thousand drawings laid bare on the tables in front of us. It was a truly staggering quantity of work. I was struck by the enormity of the task facing us, as well as a sense of hope and fragility, of our responsibility and my own inadequacy and partiality. Just a moment later, I realised that I could never hope to be impartial. There was no possibility of objective judgement, only my own personal choices and those of the other members of the jury, each with our own individual viewpoints. And in spite of our very different points of view, I felt that we all shared a similar approach, based on a respect for and attention to that enormous quantity of work, a sense of boredom with the purely decorative and exercises of style, and an awareness of just how difficult the illustrator's job is. It is a job that requires practice, humility, an ability to communicate, flexibility; an ability to look inside and beyond oneself, and to tell a story.
What I sought for amongst the thousands of illustrations was intelligence: both narrative and aesthetic. And also authenticity. I tried to steer clear of falsity, fashions and passing trends. I sought for authenticity in the use of technologies: computers used not to reproduce something that can be done better by human hands but to create something that would otherwise be unattainable. In other words, 'true' Photoshop images rather than 'false' acrylics. I looked for courage in ideas and in the search for shapes or colours. I tried to discern ability, technical skill and manual intelligence. And in the end I re-examined one by one the images that out of the thousands had remained impressed in my mind, although not all of them can be seen in this year's exhibition: a boy who kills a deer to steal its heart / a bogeyman who transforms children into obedient automata / a small and very delicately drawn chicken waiting on a bench / a very special Testament / a tangle of cut paper / a cat on a toilet / a machine for giant asparagus / very stupid geese drawn with rapid, elegant strokes / a cow drinking tea in a parlour / a world populated by terribly greedy pigs / a Little Red Riding Hood trapped in a videogame / a woman's words that slip out of her mouth like fish. This last image is perhaps the one that most accurately reflects my sensations: a lack of words. I felt the absence of that special blend of images and words that is unique to illustrated books. As if from thousands of images spread out on the tables in hall 18, the words had all of a sudden slipped away like fish. I looked for the words in the meagre captions written on the back of each of the drawings. But here, at the Illustrators Exhibition, the images have to tell their stories on their own. And we have to know how to listen to them. I don't know whether or not we have succeeded. I don't know how many genuine talents – I hope very few – have been left out of this year's catalogue and exhibition, but I am certain that some must have been. I am also certain, however, that their images will find other eyes capable of looking at them and listening to the tales they have to tell.

LISBETH ZWERGER nasce nel 1954 a Vienna, in Austria. Dal 1971 al 1974 studia Illustrazione all'Università di Arti Applicate di Vienna. Al 1976 risale il primo incontro all'Università di Linz con l'editore Friedrich Neugebauer insegnante di Calligrafia e fondatore dell'omonima casa editrice con lo scopo di lanciare giovani talenti artistici da pubblicare in belli ed esclusivi libri di illustrazioni. Il primo libro pubblicato con la Neugebauer Press è tratto dal racconto di E.T.A. Hoffmann "Das Fremde Kind". Seguono altri trenta titoli, molti dei quali pubblicati da Michael Neugebauer.

Nel corso degli anni, i suoi lavori sono stati esposti in diversi musei tra i quali il Museo del Giocattolo di Salisburgo (1979), il Museo Civico di Bologna (1990), il Kupferstichkabinett der Akademie der Bildenden Künste di Vienna (1998), il Norman Rockwell Museum nel Massachusetts (2002) e l'Eki Museum di Kyoto (2002). Numerosi premi prestigiosi le sono stati attribuiti e, nel 1990, riceve l'ambito premio Hans Christian Andersen alla carriera. Vive e lavora a Vienna.

Durante i giorni trascorsi a Bologna lo scorso gennaio, ho visto che idee brillanti erano state realizzate in modo inadeguato. E così mi sono chiesta: cosa ci vuole per migliorare la qualità delle opere inviate? Vorrei rispondere alla mia domanda e dare un suggerimento serio: migliorare il sistema scolastico! In tutto il mondo l'istruzione nel campo delle belle arti viene gravemente trascurata. Trarre ispirazione dalla natura viene considerata un'attività bizzarra e naif, un residuo del passato. Personalmente, invece, ritengo che, senza solidi fondamenti nelle competenze di base, sia molto difficile creare qualcosa di valido – e intendo qualcosa di valido di qualsiasi genere, sia nel campo dell'illustrazione che in qualsiasi altro settore. Tuttavia, anche se non avete ricevuto queste basi durante la vostra carriera scolastica, non tutto è perduto. Ecco il consiglio di zia Lisbeth: siate romantici! Portate sempre con voi un taccuino e fatevi ispirare dalla natura, come i grandi artisti del passato. Fatelo! So per esperienza che migliorerete in un batter d'occhio e in modo sorprendente!

LISBETH ZWERGER was born in 1954, in Vienna, Austria. From 1971 to 1974 she studied illustration at the University of Applied Arts in Vienna. In 1976 she first met the publisher Friedrich Neugebauer at the Art-University in Linz, where he taught Calligraphy. Friedrich Neugebauer set up his publishing house to promote talented young artists and to produce beautiful and exclusive picture books from their work. Lisbeth's first book with Neugebauer Press was E.T.A. Hoffmann's tale 'The Strange Child'. Since then she has illustrated over 30 books, nearly all of them published with Michael Neugebauer. Over the years Lisbeth Zwerger has exhibited her work in several museums, including the Toy-Museum in Salzburg (1979), the Museo Civico in Bologna (1990), the Kupferstichkabinett der Akademie der Bildenden Künste in Vienna (1998), the Norman Rockwell Museum in Massachusetts (2002) and the Eki Museum in Kyoto (2002). During her career she has been awarded several prestigious awards, and in 1990 she received the coveted Hans Christian Andersen prize for her lifetime achievement. She lives and works in Vienna.

During my days in Bologna last January, there were so many times when I saw wonderful ideas that were poorly executed. And so I asked myself: What would it take to improve on the quality of the work sent in? I would like to answer my own question and make a serious suggestion: improve the school system! All over the world, art education is being badly neglected. Drawing from nature is looked down upon as a quaint and rustic activity, a thing of the past. But personally I feel that without a solid foundation of basic skills, it is very difficult to create good work - and I mean good work of any kind, whether in illustration or any other pursuit.
But even if you missed out on this in your schooling, all is not lost. Here is Auntie Lisbeth's advice: be romantic! Always carry a small sketchbook with you and draw from nature, like the great artists of the past. Do so, and from my own experience I know that you will improve by leaps and by bounds!

Il Punto di Vista della Giuria

Si aprono le porte del Padiglione 18 della Fiera di Bologna, ed eccoci qui: lo sguardo spazia su una vasta distesa di 15.000 immagini, realizzate da circa 3.000 artisti, illustrazioni di ogni forma e dimensione, in tutte le sfumature di tutti i colori, distribuite su centinaia e centinaia di tavoli per permetterci di esaminarle. È un colpo d'occhio straordinario ma, almeno all'inizio, tutto sembra così piatto! Eppure, ciò che inizia in religioso silenzio e a due dimensioni subisce una metamorfosi nel corso delle nostre giornate di lavoro, trasformandosi in mari increspati con nuvole di spuma salata, giungle con cacofonia di verdi, città medievali intensamente immaginate... o nella topografia di un unico giardino, una panetteria, o un tavolo da pranzo come può vederlo un bambino... oppure, magari, in niente di davvero reale: nient'altro che le proiezioni astratte o simboliche dell'immaginazione di un artista. Già sul finire della prima giornata la sala silenziosa si è riempita di grida di battaglia, di spruzzi di balene, di cani abbaianti, o del suono sottile della mente umana. Oppure di un silenzio assaporato nel profondo, un silenzio con trama, colore, ottimismo, tristezza, o speranza propri.

Far parte della giuria di Bologna è un'esperienza che insegna umiltà: ci siamo sentiti profondamente ricompensati, alla fine, per aver potuto assaporare il frutto di un numero così grande di energie creative provenienti da ogni angolo del mondo. Abbiamo fatto le nostre scelte, in bella mostra, adesso, in questo meraviglioso catalogo, ma ora vogliamo restituire quanto abbiamo ricevuto dicendo a questi numerosi artisti, e anche a coloro che verranno, cosa ci ha commosso, entusiasmato, e cosa si potrebbe fare altrimenti. Avremo la possibilità di parlare direttamente con gli artisti a Bologna, nel Caffè degli Illustratori in aprile, ma possiamo già iniziare adesso...

La politica perseguita dalla Fiera consiste nel riservare lo stesso trattamento alle opere pubblicate e a quelle non pubblicate, dando ad ogni partecipante la stessa opportunità di concorrere. Non ci sono libri in mostra, né cartelle prodotte in modo lussuoso: è consentita solo qualche annotazione, di solito scritta a mano, che suggerisce le didascalie e fornisce una breve spiegazione della tecnica e del mezzo impiegati. Le cinque immagini presentate da ciascun artista, devono, quindi, parlare da sole, singolarmente ed anche in sequenza. Generalmente, ma non sempre, raccontano una storia, o quanto meno ne suggeriscono una. Che ritmo riescono a creare? Sono illustrazioni o sono semplicemente opere d'arte indipendenti, più adatte ad una galleria d'arte o alla parete di un salotto che ad illustrare una storia o a catturare l'emozione di una poesia? Suggeriscono un libro in cui voltare una pagina sia come entrare in un'altra stanza? Queste immagini sono pubblicabili come libro, ovvero, è stato scelto un mezzo riproducibile dall'editore, senza fogli in lamina d'oro o tipi di carta con trame troppo ricercate e improponibili, tagliate in forme strane? Affrontare tutto questo lavoro in un unico luogo ed in poche brevi giornate porta a numerose forme di "triage" mentale. Per prima cosa ci piace essere intrattenuti e stimolati, ma non ci piace essere annoiati. Vediamo decine di opere in stile prettamente "accademico", ma ben poche mostrano una qualche variazione personale su tale stile. Di tanto in tanto, l'opera di un artista tocca le corde del nostro inconscio: si tratta di un'opera inesplicabilmente affascinante o inquietante, ma la profondità psicologica spesso crea un legame con l'opera dell'artista che suscita forti emozioni, a prescindere dalle altre opere che vediamo.

Ci congratuliamo con i valenti artisti provenienti da tutto il mondo che hanno spedito i loro originali a Bologna: è un segno di coraggio e orgoglio ma anche di speranza e impegno. Noi, membri della Giuria degli Illustratori di questa edizione, ci auguriamo di aver ricompensato la fiducia di questi artisti con la selezione da parte nostra di una gamma ampia e ricca di opere da esporre e che la mostra che ne scaturisce sia fonte di ispirazione per coloro che vorranno partecipare l'anno prossimo e intervenire nel dibattito sul futuro delle illustrazioni dei libri per ragazzi.

The View from the Jury

The doors in Hall 18 of the Bologna fairgrounds open and there we stand, gazing over a vast plain of 15,000 images by close to 3,000 artists, pictures of all shapes and sizes, in all shades of all colors, distributed over hundreds and hundreds of tables for our review. It is an astonishing vista. And - at first at least - everything is so flat! Yet what begins in awed silence and in two dimensions metamorphoses over the days of our work into undulating seas with clouds of salty spume, cacophonous green jungles, densely imagined medieval cities... or into the topography of a single garden, a bakery, or a dinner table as a child might experience it... or perhaps into nothing real at all: only the abstract or symbolic projections of an artist's imagination. Already, by the end of the first day, the silent room has been filled with cries of battle, of whales spouting, dogs barking, or with the subtle music of the human mind. Or just a profoundly experienced silence, a silence with its own texture, color, optimism, sadness, or hope.

It is a humbling experience, serving on the Bologna jury. We feel so richly rewarded by the end, to have been able to savor the fruits of so many creative energies from all corners of the world. We've made our choices - which are arrayed now in this beautiful catalog -and now we want to give back, tell these many artists, and those yet to come, what has moved us, pleased us, and what might be done differently. We will have a chance to speak with the artists directly in Bologna in the Illustrators Café in April, but let us make a start now...

It is the policy of the fair that published and unpublished works are treated the same, giving every participant the same chance to compete. There are no books on display, no lavishly produced dossiers - only a few notes are possible, usually handwritten, proposing captions and providing a brief statement of technique and medium used. The five pictures each artist submits, therefore, must speak for themselves, individually and also in sequence. Normally, but not always, they tell a story or at least suggest one. What dramatic rhythm do they create? Are they illustrations, or are they just free-standing pieces of art, more suitable for a gallery or a living room wall than to illustrate a story or capture the mood of a poem? Do they suggest a book, one in which turning a page is like entering another room? And are these images publishable as a book, which is to say or to ask: Is the medium chosen reproducible by a publisher without sheets of gold leaf or unaffordable highly textured papers cut into strange shapes?

Facing all this work in one place and in a few short days leads to many forms of mental triage. For one, we enjoy being entertained and excited. We don't like being bored. We see dozens of works in academy styles, fewer works that show individual variations on these styles. Every so often an artist's work resonates in our subconscious: it is either inexplicably delightful or disturbing, but psychological depth frequently creates a bond with an artist's work that results in enormous sympathies, regardless what else we might be seeing.

We congratulate the talented artists from all over the world who submitted their original works to Bologna. This reflects courage and pride as well as hope and commitment. For our parts, we of this year's Illustrators Jury hope we have rewarded these artists' confidence in the process of selection by choosing a broad and rich group of works for display - for an exhibit which may inspire other artists to participate next year, joining an important conversation about the future of children's book illustration.

Illustratori Selezionati
Selected Illustrators

Fiction

A
Amekan Hassan 26/*203*
Aoki Yuko 28/*203*
Arakawa Keiko 30/*203*

B
Behnzadi Azad Behnoush 32/*204*
Bolis Francesca 34/*204*
Bongibault Jennifer 36/*205*
Boozari Ali 36/*205*
Bourgon Mathilde 40/*206*
Bräuning Lotte 42/*206*

C
Carls Claudia 44/*206*
Carvalho André 46/*207*
Cavallini Valentina 48/*207*
Ceccoli Nicoletta 50/*208*
Celija Maja 52/*208*
Chattellard Isabelle 54/*208*
Chausson Julia 56/*209*
Cleminson Katie 58/*209*

F
Forgione Biagio 60/*210*
Fulvi Marianna 62/*210*

G
Gnosspelius Staffan 64/*211*
Gorni Roberta 66/*211*

J
Jun Tan 68/*212*

K
Kainz Franz 70/*212*
Kamino Saori 72/*212*
Kárpáti Tibor 74/*213*
Karrebaek Dorte 76/*213*
Kheirieh Rashin 78/*213*
Kim Suk-Kyoung 80/*214*
Kimura Harumi 82/*214*
Kubo Takayuki 84/*214*

L
Leboeuf Arthur 86/*215*
Lecis Alessandro 88/*215*
Lima Teresa 90/*215*
Longaretti D./Tazumi M. 92/*216*

M
Mahmoodi Golnaz 94/*216*
Makhult Gabriella 96/*216*
Mendonça Gemeo Luis 98/*217*
Misfeldt Anne/Stamp Jørgen 100/*217*
Morri Stefano 102/*218*

N
Nagano Hiroshi 104/*218*
Nagano Junko 106/*218*
Nakayama Ely 108/*219*
Nanni Lisa 110/*219*
Neubert Franziska 112/*219*
Noda Yoshiko 114/*220*

O
Obata Kumi 116/*220*
Offerman Andrea 118/*220*
Oyama Kazuko 120/*221*

P

Pacheco Gabriel 122/*221*
Panzeri Alessandra 124/*221*
Park Yeon-Cheol 126/*222*
Pflüeger Lena 128/*222*
Pintor David 130/*223*
Pizzo Fulvia 132/*223*
Poirot Cherif Sandra 134/*223*
Pollet Clémence 136/*224*

Q

Maurizio Quarello 138/*224*

R

Raffaelli Luigi 140/*224*
Rossin Fabio Ramiro 142/*225*
Rastatter Linda 144/*225*
Raud Piret 146/*225*

S

Sadat Mandana 148/*226*
Sanna Alessandro 150/*226*
Satoh Masanobu 152/*226*
Shaabanipour Amir 154/*227*
Sommer Marie 156/*228*
Sonoda Erie 158/*228*
Sparke Franki 160/*228*
Stuhrmann Jochen 162/*229*

T

Tanaka Yoko 164/*229*
Tsai Ta-Yuan 166/*229*
Tsuritani Kouki 168/*230*

Z

Zumbé Marco 170/*231*

Non Fiction

B

Ballestra Giovanni 174/*204*
Bonacina Irène 176/*205*

C

Calciolari Guglielmo 178/*207*

D

Donaera Patrizia 180/*209*

G

Garnier François 182/*210*
Guarneri Cedric 184/*211*

M

Miura Taro 186/*217*

P

Pierazzi Mitri Monica 188/*222*

S

Shiozawa Tomomi 190/*227*
Siems Annika 192/*227*

Z

Zagnoli Olimpia 194/*230*
Zhilichkin Pyotr 196/*230*

FICTION

Hassan Amekan
Iran

Title of Work
Wonder City

Technique
Mixed

Captions
· *A big fish who lived in this city disturbed a little fish*
· *Once upon a time a big-hat man riding a bicycle came into a fish city*
· *One day a big-hat man was hunting a big fish. He flew with it, then the animal attacked him*

Yuko Aoki
Japan

Title of Work
The Joys of Living

Technique
Copperplate engraving

Captions
· *The joy of spouting*
· *Morning joy – Breakfast with the mouse*
· *The joy of returning – Home sweet home*

KEIKO ARAKAWA
Japan

Title of Work
Rosey and a Good Friend

Technique
Etching

Captions
· *When I go out and do it, I am the same as Rosey*
· *Rosey bloomed with a flower*
· *I met Rosey in a flower shop*
· *I read a book for Rosey*
· *Rosey on a rainy day*

Behnoush Behnzadi Azad
Iran

Title of Work
Last Night I Dreamed of my Father in Reality

Technique
Mixed

Captions
· *Sometimes look at the sky*
· *Step by step to meet the mother*

Francesca Bolis
Italy

Title of Work
Beyond the Garden

Technique
Acrylic, collage

Captions
· *The red carpet*
· *On the edge of time*
· *Growth*

Jennifer Bongibault
France

Title of Work
Migration

Technique
Screen printing, ink

Captions
· *Migration 1*
· *Migration 3*
· *Migration 4*
· *Migration 5*

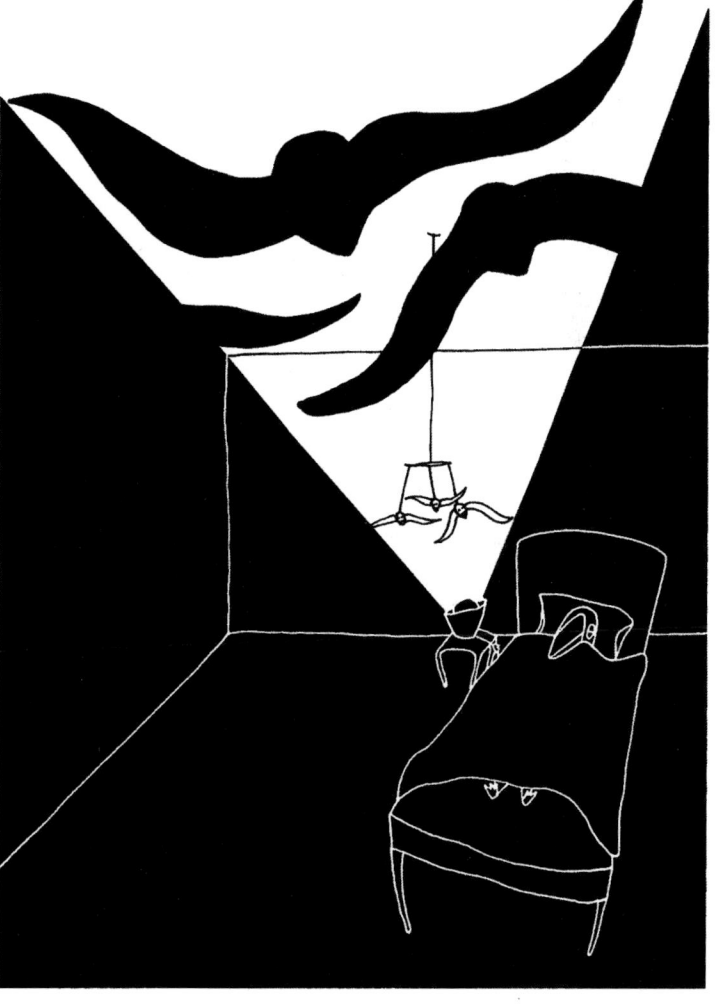

ALI BOOZARI
Iran

Title of Work
The Land of Water-Lilies

Original Publisher and Date of Publication
Shabaviz Publishing Co.
Tehran 2006
ISBN 964 505 202 5

Technique
Mixed

Captions
- The young king went to the tree but it was more like a jungle than a tree
- Once upon a time there lived a young king who wished to have the happiest people in his country

MATHILDE BOURGON
France

Title of Work
The day I got chickenpox

Technique
Screen printing

Captions
· *I was sitting quietly*
· *Then they changed*

Lotte Bräuning
Germany

Title of Work
Shadows

Technique
Pencil, acrylic

Captions
· *Cover*
· *The town*

CARLS CLAUDIA
Germany

Title of Work
The Cauldron

Technique
Photos of small clay sculptures, digitally combined with computer-coloured pencil drawings

Captions
· *The prince and the Miller's daughter*
· *The journey*

ANDRÉ CARVALHO
Portugal

Title of Work
Meia Bola

*Original Publisher
and Date of Publication*
Edições Éterogémeas
Porto, 2006
ISBN 972 99243 6 8

Technique
Acrylic, stencil

Captions
· There she goes…
· Can I take a photo?
· Click!

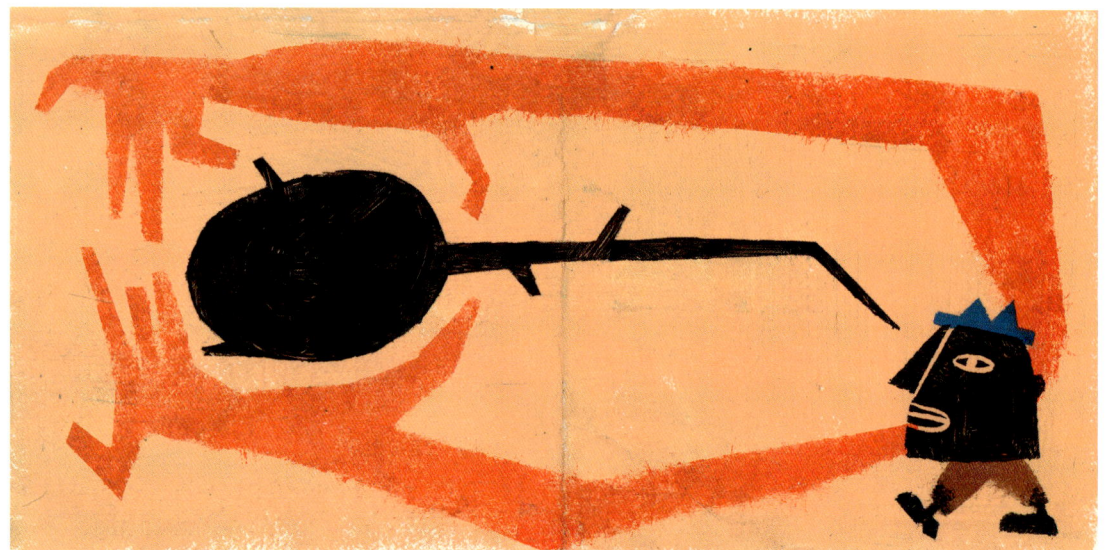

Valentina Cavallini
Italy

Title of Work
Choose a Number, Ollie!

Technique
Collage, digital

Captions
· On the seventh day he went back and the big bird was still there, as though hypnotized by the song of the river
· He whistled his song and from the woods a mysterious voice replied…

Nicoletta Ceccoli
Republic of San Marino

Title of Work
Untitled

Captions
· *Spider-girl*
· *Mermaids*

Technique
Acrylic, Photoshop

Maja Celija
Slovenia

Title of Work
Chiuso per Ferie

**Original Publisher
and Date of Publication**
Topipittori
Milan, 2006
ISBN 88 89210 10 9

Technique
Acrylic on paper

Captions
· Skates as cars
· The dog is chased by
  mosquitoes

Isabelle Chattelard
France

Title of Work
L'ours de Noël

Original Publisher and Date of Publication
Editions Bilboquet, 2006
ISBN 2 84181 253 7

Technique
Acrylic, charcoal

Captions
· I peep out of the bag
· The mice will take care of me

Julia Chausson
France

Title of Work
The Knights

Technique
Etching on wood, two and three colour technique

Captions
· *The apparition*
· *The bloodbath*
· *Waging war*

KATIE CLEMINSON
Great Britain

Title of Work
What's Inside Animals?

Technique
Mixed media

Captions
· Hang ten
· Russian doll rabbit
· Flying out trunks

Biagio Forgione
Italy

Title of Work
In the Bottom of the Bucket

Technique
Acrylic on paper

Captions
· *Below in the darkness*
· *The devourer*

Marianna Fulvi
Italy

Title of Work
Exit

Technique
Digital

Captions
· *Red the thinker*
· *Flashback*
· *The great escape*
· *"What a terrible fright!!"*

STAFFAN GNOSSPELIUS
Sweden

Title of Work
Julia and The Triple C

Technique
Colourgraph prints

Captions
· *Waiting for the uncle*
· *Are we there yet?*

ROBERTA GORNI
Italy

Title of Work
Elia non vuole andare a letto

*Original Publisher
and Date of Publication*
Edizioni Fatatrac
Florence, 2005
ISBN 88 8222 127 X

Technique
Acrylic, pencil, pastel

Captions
· *Running away*
· *Chatting on the bed*
· *Warm bread*
· *Wake up Elia!*

TAN JUN
China

Title of Work
The daughter mouse's wedding

Technique
Charcoal, Acrylic, Tea, Papers, Ink

Captions
- *But the cloud is afraid of the wind and the wind is afraid of the wall*
- *In the end his daughter marries a handsome mouse*

Franz Kainz
Austria

Title of Work
About Living Together

Technique
Ink, watercolours

Captions
· *The visit to the city*
· *My neighbours, the elephants*

Heute endlich fuhr mein Freund, das Krokodil mit mir in die Stadt. Meine Tante hatte uns nämlich erzählt, daß man in der Stadt nie mit leerem Magen zu Bett gehen müsse, weil es dort nur so vor Menschen wimmeln soll. Jetzt fuhren wir aber schon seit einer geschlagenen Stunde kreuz und quer durch die Stadt und haben immer noch keine Menschenseele gesehen. Ich glaube, meine Tante hat uns einen Bären aufgebunden. Na, der werde ich aber etwas erzählen, wenn wir wieder zu Hause sind!

Meine Nachbarn, die Elefanten, sind eigentlich ganz nett.

Nur wenn sie tanzen,
die Elefanten,
tanzt mein Geschirr
und mir wird ganz bange,
um meine Teller und Tassen.

SAORI KAMINO
Japan

Title of Work
Omu-rice Baron

Technique
Acrylic, gouache

Captions
· Let's eat this omu-rice
· Omu-rice baron said "Who are you?"
· Omu-rice baron helps a lady
· "Repair the wall by tomorrow morning"

Tibor Kárpáti
Hungary

Title of Work
Piroska és a farkas

Original Publisher and Date of Publication
Csimota, 2006
ISBN 9 799638 635098

Technique
Computer

DORTE KARREBAEK
Denmark

Title of Work
De Tre Nr II - da Carlo blev bidt midt over af en stor, stor hund

Original Publisher and Date of Publication
Dansklaerforeningens Forlag, 2006
ISBN 87 7996 217 3

Technique
Watercolour, Ink

Captions
· Sima
· Carlo

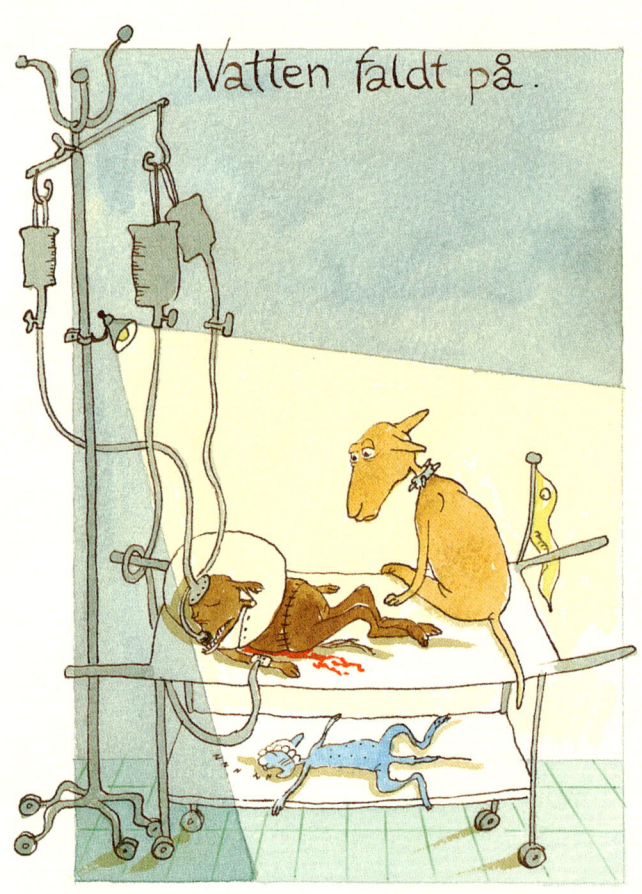

Rashin Kheirieh
Iran

Title of Work
The Stupid Geese

Technique
Linoleum

Captions
- One of the geese flies away
- The landlord has chosen the fat ones
- When the geese were in the water

SUK-KYOUNG KIM
Republic of Korea

Title of Work
Lucky Pig at the Street Corner

Original Publisher and Date of Publication
Darim Publishing Co., 2006
ISBN 89 87721 86 8

Technique
Collage on tracing paper

Captions
· *Watching pigs*
· *Pursuing luck*

HARUMI KIMURA
Japan

Title of Work
The Hope

Technique
Mixed

Captions
· *Sometimes, it flows like the air between one person and another*
· *To give someone the strength to live*

TAKAYUKI KUBO
Japan

Title of Work
It Searches for my House

Technique
Mezzotint

Captions
· *Higher place*
· *Life of two sheep*
· *Driven out by full occupancy*

Arthur Leboeuf
France

Title of Work
Pinocchio

Technique
Gouache

Caption
· *Bad faith*

ALESSANDRO LECIS
Italy

Title of Work
Metamorphosis

Technique
Collage, digital

Captions
· *Dragonfly-balloons*
· *Frogship*
· *Snailplanes*
· *Squid-submarine*

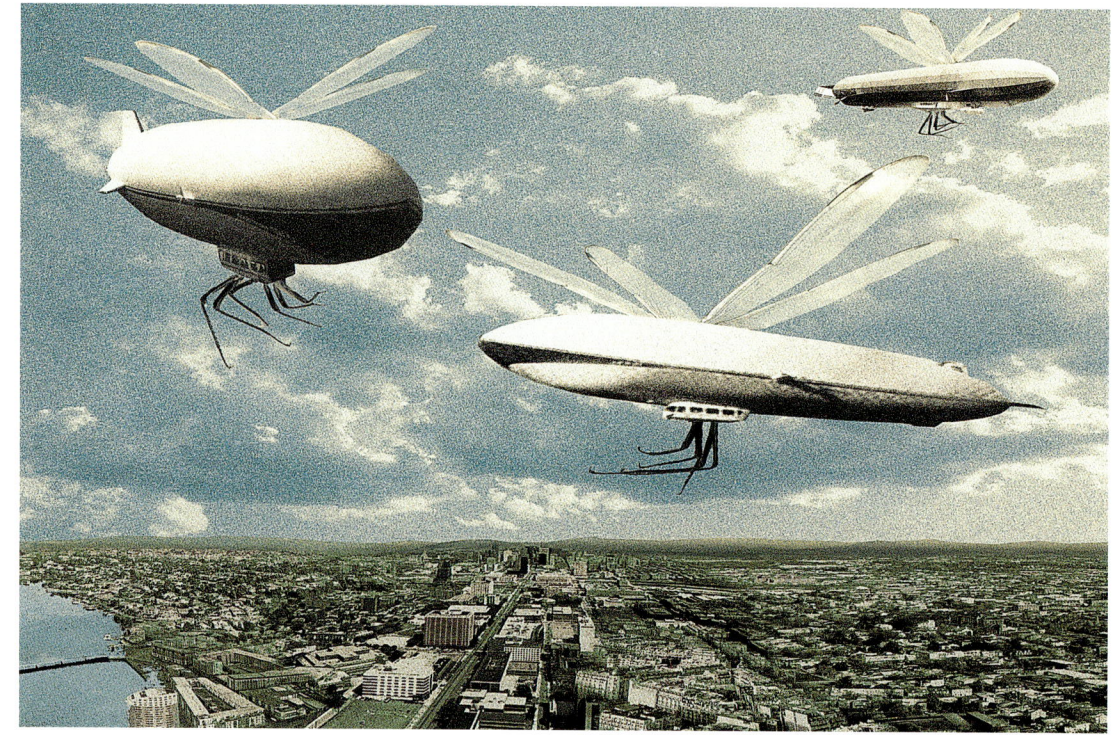

Teresa Lima
Portugal

Title of Work
Histórias de animais de Rudyard Kipling

Original Publisher and Date of Publication
Ambar Editora
Porto, 2006
ISBN 972 43 0913 4

Technique
Mixed

Captions
· Darzee and his wife
· Rikki-tikki-tavi

DAVIDE LONGARETTI – MAYUKO TAZUMI
Italy - Japan

Title of Work
Urashimataro

Technique
Mixed
(plasticine, computer)

Captions
· Back home: everything changed
· Taro saves a turtle from kids
· The queen of sea's gift

GOLNAZ MAHMOODI
Iran

Title of Work
The Last Dream of the Old Oak

Technique
Mixed

Captions
· *Death of the fly*
· *The tree felt itself stretch*
· *Dance of tiny creatures*
· *The tree's hearing*

GABRIELLA MAKHULT
Hungary

Title of Work
Poems of Kányádi Sándor for Children

Technique
Linocut, mixed, colour paper

Captions
· The goat accidentally broke down a fence in the market…
· The boy is walking on the hill, evening comes…
· There was a man, who was sitting on the tree…
· It is still autumn, but the crows are already coming

GÉMEO LUÍS MENDONÇA
Portugal

Title of Work
ABeCé de Las Historias

Original Publisher and Date of Publication
Edições Éterogémeas
Porto, 2005
ISBN 972 99243 4 1

Technique
Craft paper cutting

Captions
· ABC of stories 2
· ABC of stories 4

ANNE MISFELDT – JØRGEN STAMP

Denmark

Title of Work
"Flyv" & "Kør"

Original Publisher and Date of Publication
Forlaget Carlsen
Copenhagen, 2006
ISBN 87 626 5147 1
ISBN 87 626 5146 3

Technique
Collage

Captions
· *In front of/behind*
· *Wet/dry*
· *Up/down*

STEFANO MORRI
Italy

Title of Work
Cappuccetto Rosso

Original Publisher and Date of Publication
Edizioni Arka
Milan, 2006
ISBN 88 8072 161 5

Technique
Mixed, computer

Hiroshi Nagano
Japan

Title of Work
Gaburi

Technique
Watercolour

Captions
· *Gaburi*
· *Gaburi*

JUNKO NAGANO
Japan

Title of Work
The Fantasy in my Book

Technique
Etching, coloured pencil

Captions
· *The fantasy in my book will last forever*
· *Prologue. In the underground collection room*

Ely Nakayama
Brazil

Title of Work
Houses for All

Technique
Acrylic on paper

Captions
· Mole lives in a warm house
· A cosy house for four

LISA NANNI
Italy

Title of Work
Alice

Technique
Pastels, acrylic

Captions
· *Run away White Rabbit*
· *There's a dormouse in the teapot*
· *In the rabbit's house*

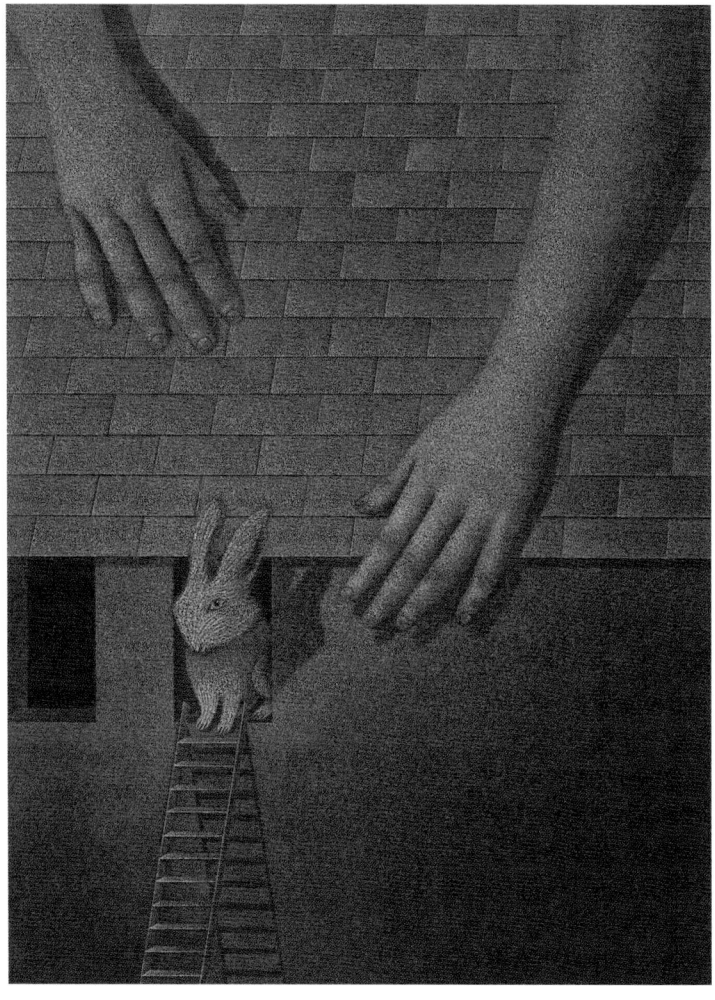

Franziska Neubert
Germany

Title of Work
Rue Blanche

Technique
Etching

Captions
· Market
· Night
· The Café

YOSHIKO NODA
Japan

Title of Work
Little Piglet

Technique
Pen, Ink

Captions
· A little piglet is born
· He swims in the orangeade lake with his mother
· He goes up to the castle via the pencil staircase with his father
· He counts the number of leaves he has spread strawberry jam on with his grandparents

Kumi Obata
Japan

Title of Work
The Place with a Treasure

Technique
Etching

Captions
· *Sweet-smelling wind blows*
· *Where beautiful music comes from*

ANDREA OFFERMAN
Germany

Title of Work
Life of Pi

Technique
Pen, ink, oil, digital

Captions
- *The ship sank*
- *I would be visited by the most extraordinary dreams*

KAZUKO OYAMA
Japan

Title of Work
Travel in Summer

Technique
Computer graphics

Captions
· Little accident
· It is hungry
· Play in the sea
· One's favourite song

Gabriel Pacheco
Mexico

Title of Work
La llave de oro y otros cuentos

Original Publisher and Date of Publication
Editorial Anaya
La Coruña 2006
ISBN 84 667 5386 9

Technique
Digital computer

Captions
· The goose keeper
· The drummer

ALESSANDRA PANZERI
Italy

Title of Work
Animators

Technique
Mixed

Captions
· *Questioners*
· *Branchers*

YEAN-CHEOL PARK
Republic of Korea

Title of Work
Bogeymen is Coming

Original Publisher and Date of Publication
Sigongsa Co., Ltd.
Seoul, 2007
ISBN 978 89 527 4864 5

Technique
Printmaking, computer

Caption
· *Strange sound outside*

Lena Pflüger
Germany

Title of Work
The Monsters' Parade

Technique
Mixed media

Captions
· The fantastic parade
· The defender of the castle
· The rebellious Ocelot

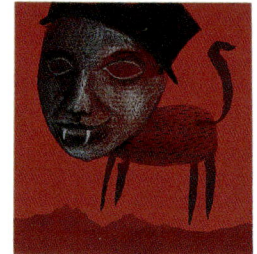

DAVID PINTOR
Spain

Title of Work
Santorini

Technique
Ink, computer

Captions
· *Venice*
· *Prague I*

FULVIA PIZZO
Italy

Titles of Work
My Creatures

Technique
Acrylic on canvas

Captions
· *Happiness*
· *Arguing*

Sandra Poirot Cherif
France

Title of Work
Grandir

Original Publisher and Date of Publication
Editions Fleurus
Paris, 2005
ISBN 2 215 07748 4

Technique
Acrylic, collage

Captions
· Listen to me
· Too difficult

CLÉMENCE POLLET
France

Title of Work
Crazy About Asparagus

Technique
Watercolour, pen, collage, colour pencils

Captions
· *Building the asparagus machine*
· *Cultivate the asparagus field*

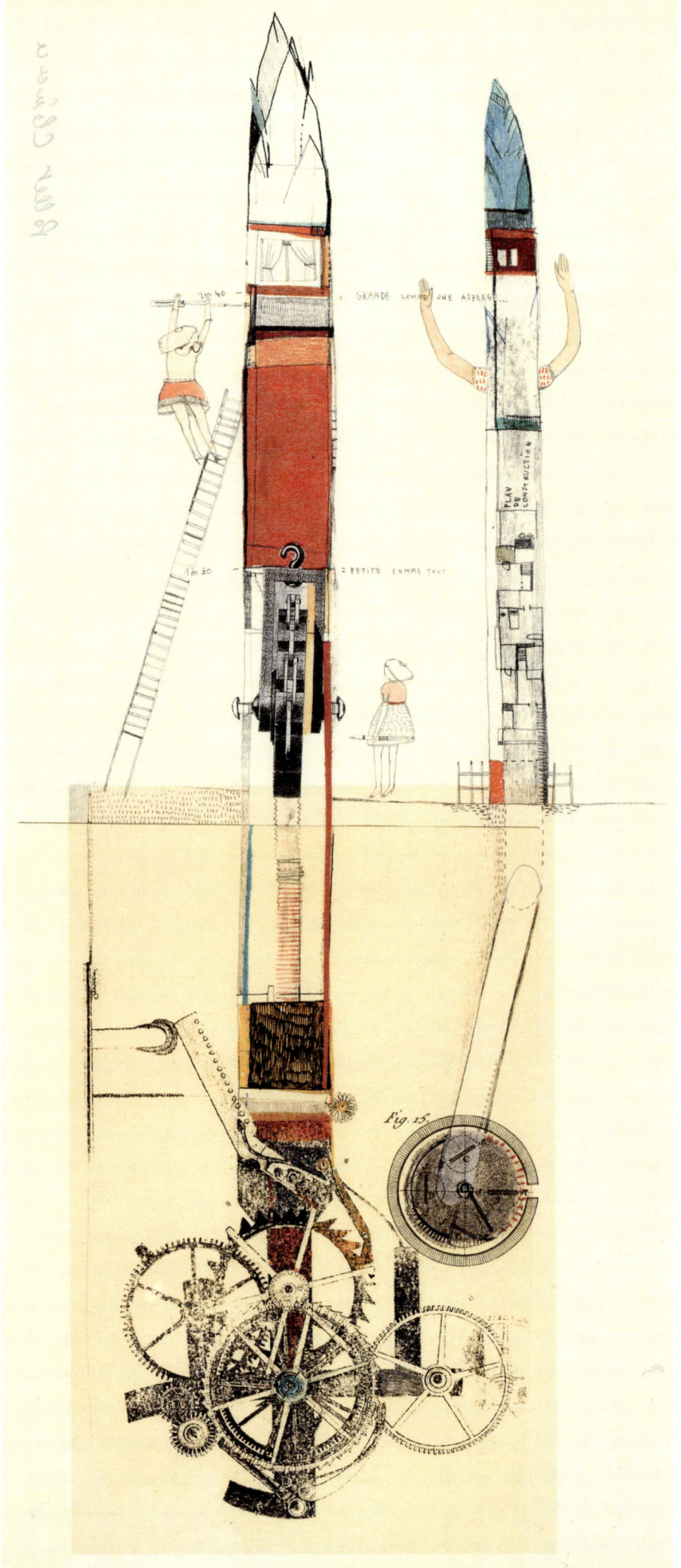

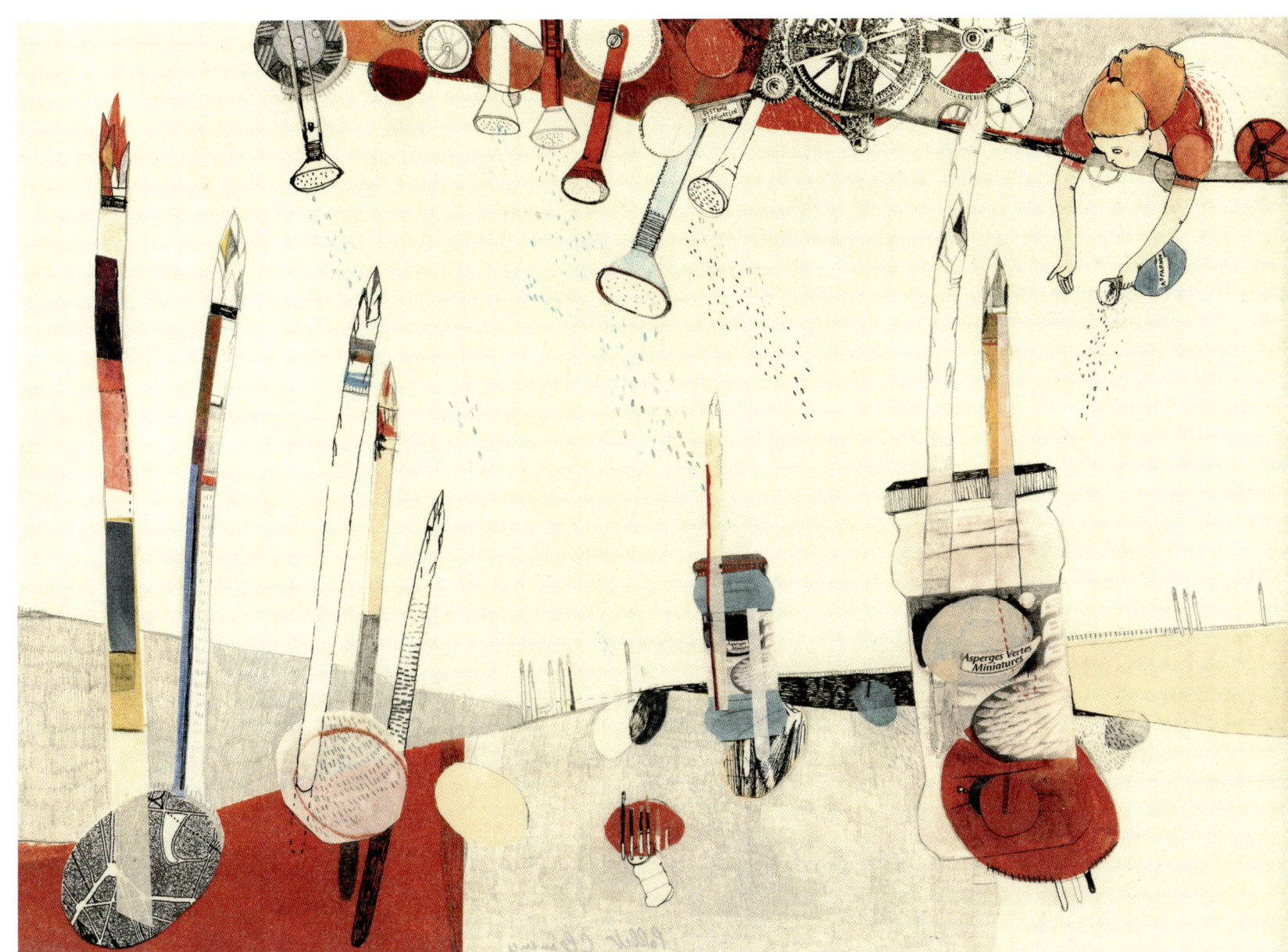

MAURIZIO QUARELLO
Italy

Title of Work
Toni Mannaro Jazz Band

Original Publisher and Date of Publication
Orecchio Acerbo Edizioni
Rome, 2006
ISBN 88 89025 34 4

Technique
Acrylic, mixed

Captions
· *Toni and the bouncers*
· *Carmine Mole*

LUIGI RAFFAELLI
Italy

Title of Work
Storie del Terzo Millennio

*Original Publisher
and Date of Publication*
Campanotto Ragazzi
Pasian di Prato, UD 2006
ISBN 88 456 0778 X

Technique
Acrylic on paper

Captions
· M.A.I.
· Invention of the cube
· The last Tyrannosauri

FABIO RAMIRO ROSSIN
Italy

Title of Work
Testament

Technique
Acrylic, pen on canvas

Captions
· *Original sin*
· *Sodom*
· *The flood*
· *Annunciation*
· *Temptation*

LINDA RASTATTER
Hungary

Title of Work
The Silly Adult

Technique
Acrylic

Captions
· *Dorottya is getting over the tantrum*
· *Bat ping-pong*
· *Dorottya, the leader*

145

Piret Raud
Estonia

Title of Work
Fables

Technique
Indian Ink, watercolour

Captions
· *The Hound and the Hare*
· *The Fox and the Stork*
· *The Elephant and the Jackals*

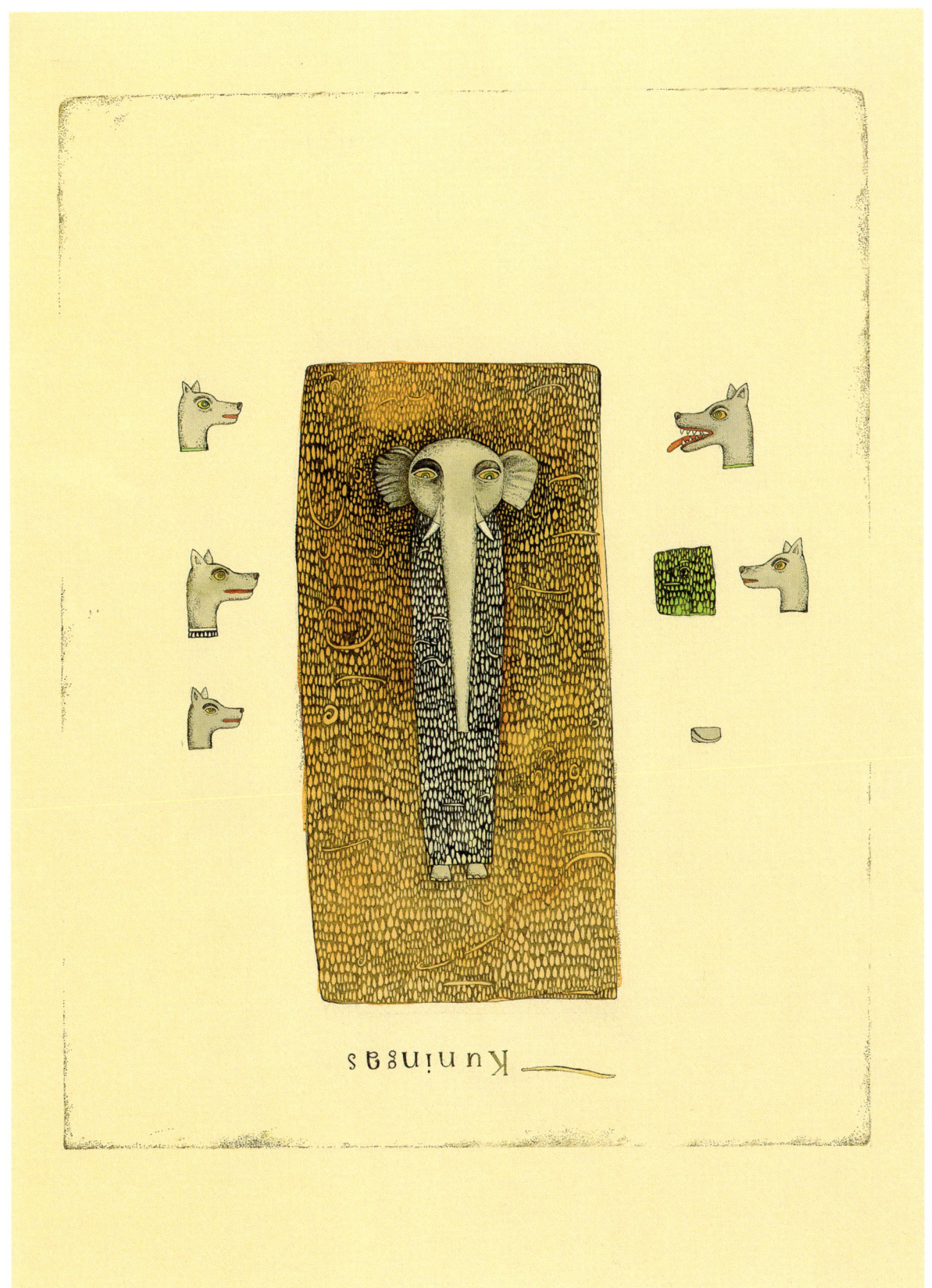

MANDANA SADAT
Belgium

Title of Work
Cosas con plumas

Original Publisher and Date of Publication
Editorial Kókinos
Madrid, 2006
ISBN 84 88342 92 6

Technique
Mixed, computer

Captions
· "Who are you?", "I am myself.", "What are you carrying there?", "My ideas."
· " Would you exchange one with one of mine?", " With pleasure."

ALESSANDRO SANNA
Italy

Title of Work
Bestiary

Technique
Watercolour

Captions
· *Lion*
· *Elephant*
· *Antelope*
· *Crocodile*

Masanobu Satoh
Japan

Title of Work
One Day of Mr. Spectacles

Technique
Acrylic resin

Captions
· *Get up*
· *Gather up the water*
· *Time for tea*
· *Clean up*

Amir Shaabanipour
Iran

Title of Work
The Fox

Original Publisher and Date of Publication
Shabaviz Publishing Co.
Tehran, 2006
ISBN 964 505 210 6

Technique
Mixed

Captions
· The hencoop was a wooden cabin and I could easily enter it
· I tried to creep out of the gap but I saw the red eyes and giant teeth of the dog

Marie Sommer
France

Title of Work
Wolf, try to catch us!

Technique
Etching

Captions
· At the table
· Playing chess

Erie Sonoda
Japan

Title of Work
Don't Ask Why

Technique
Pencil, pastel

Captions
· *The last bus has gone…*
· *Can you give me a lift?*
· *(say nothing)*

Franki Sparke
Australia

Title of Work
Wherever you go –
There you are

Technique
Stamped relief-print, gouache

Captions
· *Another place*
· *Wherever you go –
There you are*

WHEREVER YOU GO
THERE YOU ARE

JOCHEN STUHRMANN
Germany

Title of Work
Dogs at Work

Technique
Acrylic on paper

Captions
· Track Hounds
· Sales Mastiff
· Flying Dogs

Yoko Tanaka
Japan

Title of Work
Theodosia and the Serpents of Chaos

Technique
Acrylic glazing

Captions
· *At Charing Cross Station*
· *Under the moonlight*
· *Nap in the sarcophagus*
· *"I'm finally here"*

Ta-Yuan Tsai
Taiwan

Title of Work
Tian-Ding Liao The Legend

Technique
Watercolour, coloured pencil

Captions
· *Manhunt*
· *Almsgiving*

Kouki Tsuritani
Japan

Title of Work
Little Red Riding Hood

Technique
Mezzotint

Captions
· *She made bouquets*
· *"Go, my dear"*
· *The Wolf ate her up in a moment*

Marco Zumbè
Germany

Title of Work
Braveheart

Technique
Scratchboard, Photoshop

Captions
· Shot
· Gift
· Awake

NON FICTION

GIOVANNI BALLESTRA
Italy

Title of Work
Relics

Technique
Watercolour

Captions
· *Skeleton coast*
· *Aral Lake 1*

BONACINA IRÈNE
France

Title of Work
Hybrids

Technique
Black Ink

Captions
· *Nuptial parades*
· *Inventory of species*

GUGLIELMO CALCIOLARI
Italy

Title of Work
Architecture reconstruction

Technique
Ink

Caption
· Mantua in the Middle Ages (1402)

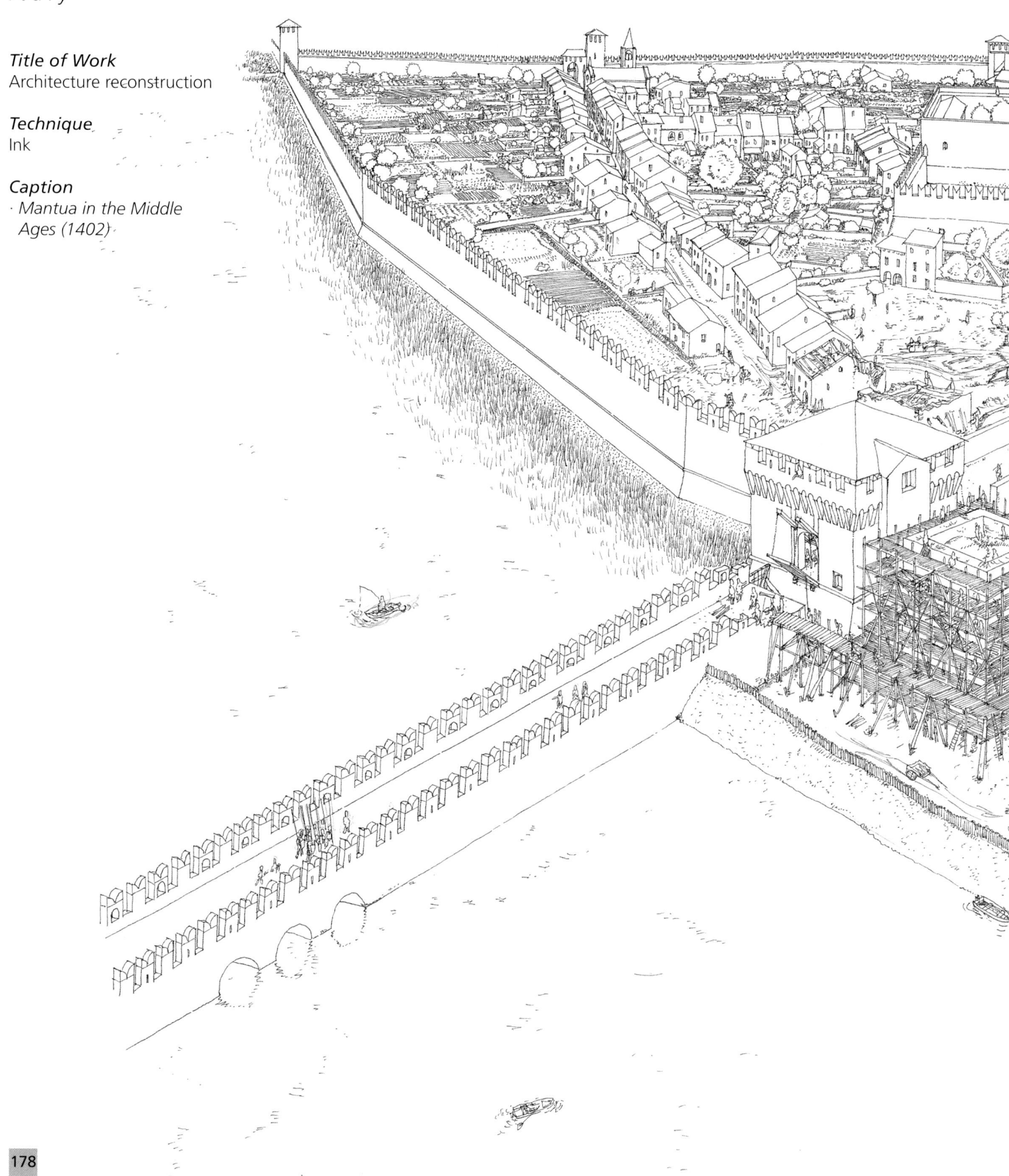

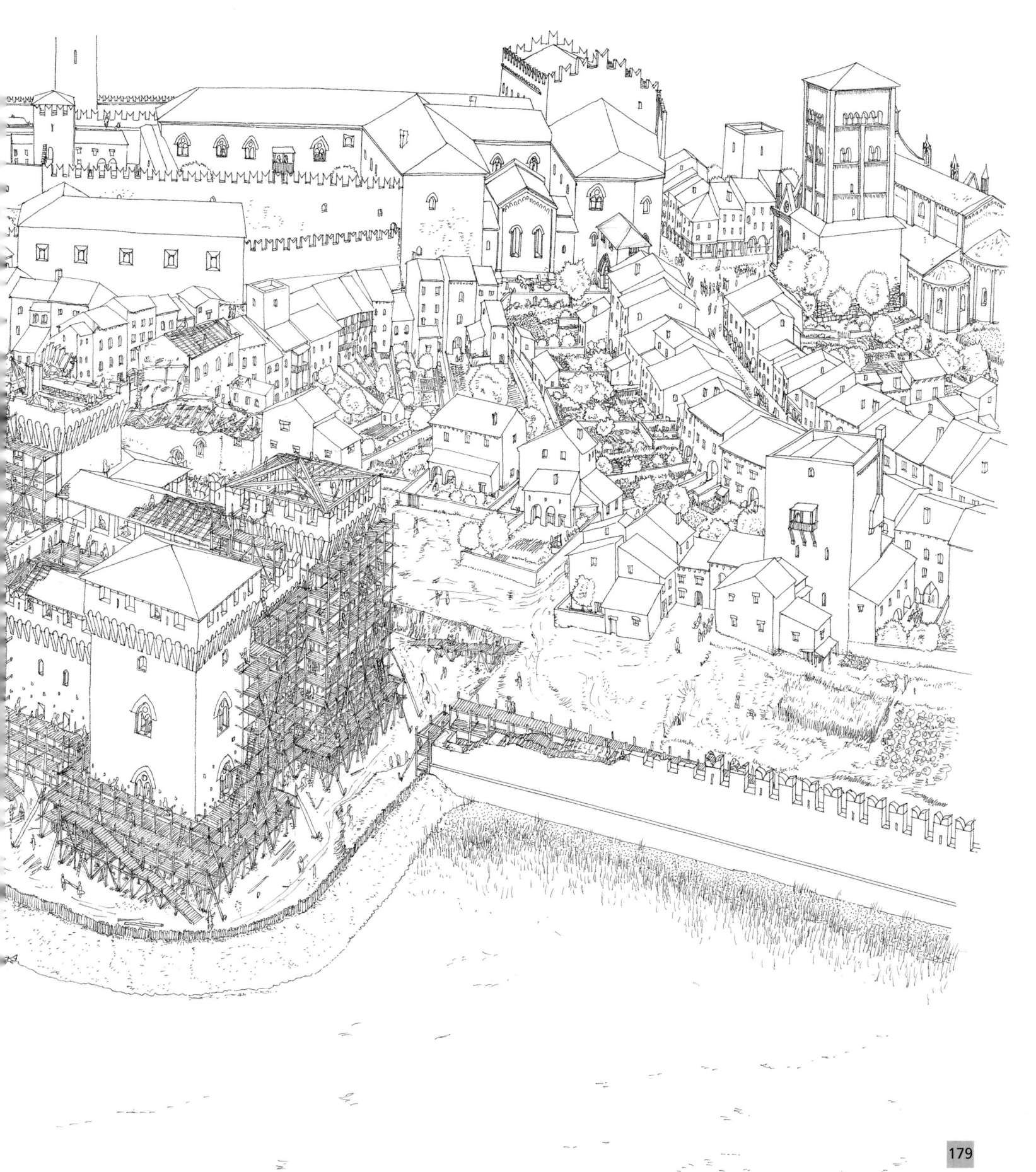

Patrizia Donaera
Italy

Title of Work
Watch Them Grow.
Who's Hatching?

**Original Publisher
and Date of Publication**
Pinwheel Limited
London, 2007
ISBN 978 1 86199 136 2

Technique
Watercolour

Captions
· Penguin steps
· Duck steps
· Turtle steps

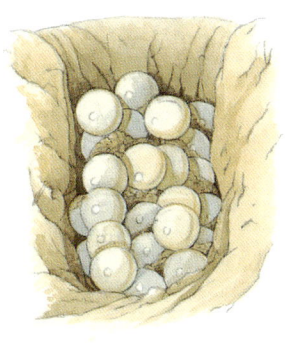

François Garnier
France

Title of Work
Imminence

Technique
Mixed

Captions
- It's the things we don't understand that we like to explain
- Those who run from danger dare not wait for it
- We're more in danger of being crushed when we've just dodged a car
- Fate triumphs as soon as we believe in its existence

C'EST SURTOUT CE QU'ON NE COMPREND PAS QU'ON EXPLIQUE.
(Barbey d'Aurevilly (Jules))

TEL COURT AU DANGER QUI N'OSERAIT L'ATTENDRE.
(Duc de Lévis)

ON EST LE PLUS EN DANGER D'ÊTRE ÉCRASÉ LORSQU'ON VIENT D'ESQUIVER UNE VOITURE.
[Friedrich Nietzsche]

[...] LA FATALITÉ TRIOMPHE DÈS QU'ON CROIT EN ELLE.
[Beauvoir (Simone de)]

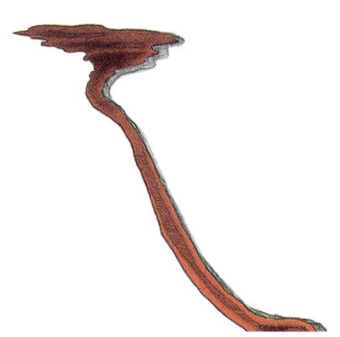

Cédric Guarneri
France

Titles of Works
Mixed Animals

Technique
Acrylic, linocut

Captions
· *Chain snake*
· *Key Fish*
· *Staple insect*

Taro Miura
Japan

Title of Work
Lavori in corso

Original Publisher and Date of Publication
Corraini Edizioni
Mantua, 2007
ISBN 978 88 7570 100 0

Technique
Computer graphics

Captions
· GRRRR!!!
· VRRR! VRRR! CLANG!
· VRRRR!

Monica Pierazzi Mitri
Italy

Title of Work
Animal Faces

Technique
Etching

Captions
· Cow
· Dog

Tomomi Shiozawa
Japan

Title of Work
The Creatures

Technique
Watercolour, pen

Caption
· Ocean Fishes

Annika Siems
Germany

Title of Work
Animals

Technique
Acrylic, oil

Captions
· *Flamingos*
· *Chameleon*

Olimpia Zagnoli
Italy

Title of Work
The Anatomy of Tissue Paper

Technique
Mixed media

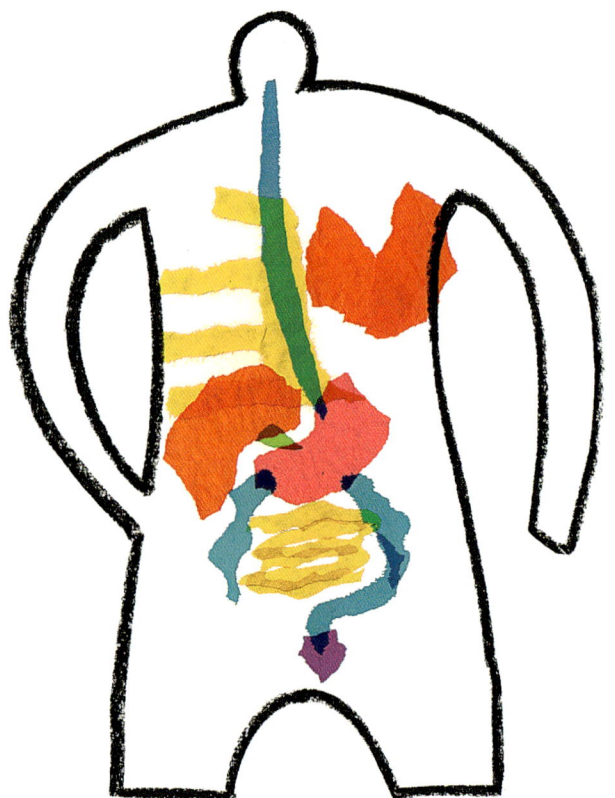
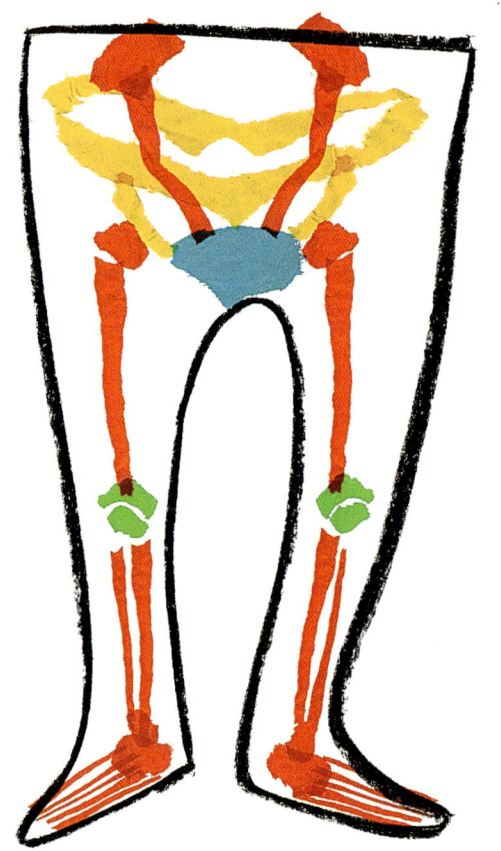

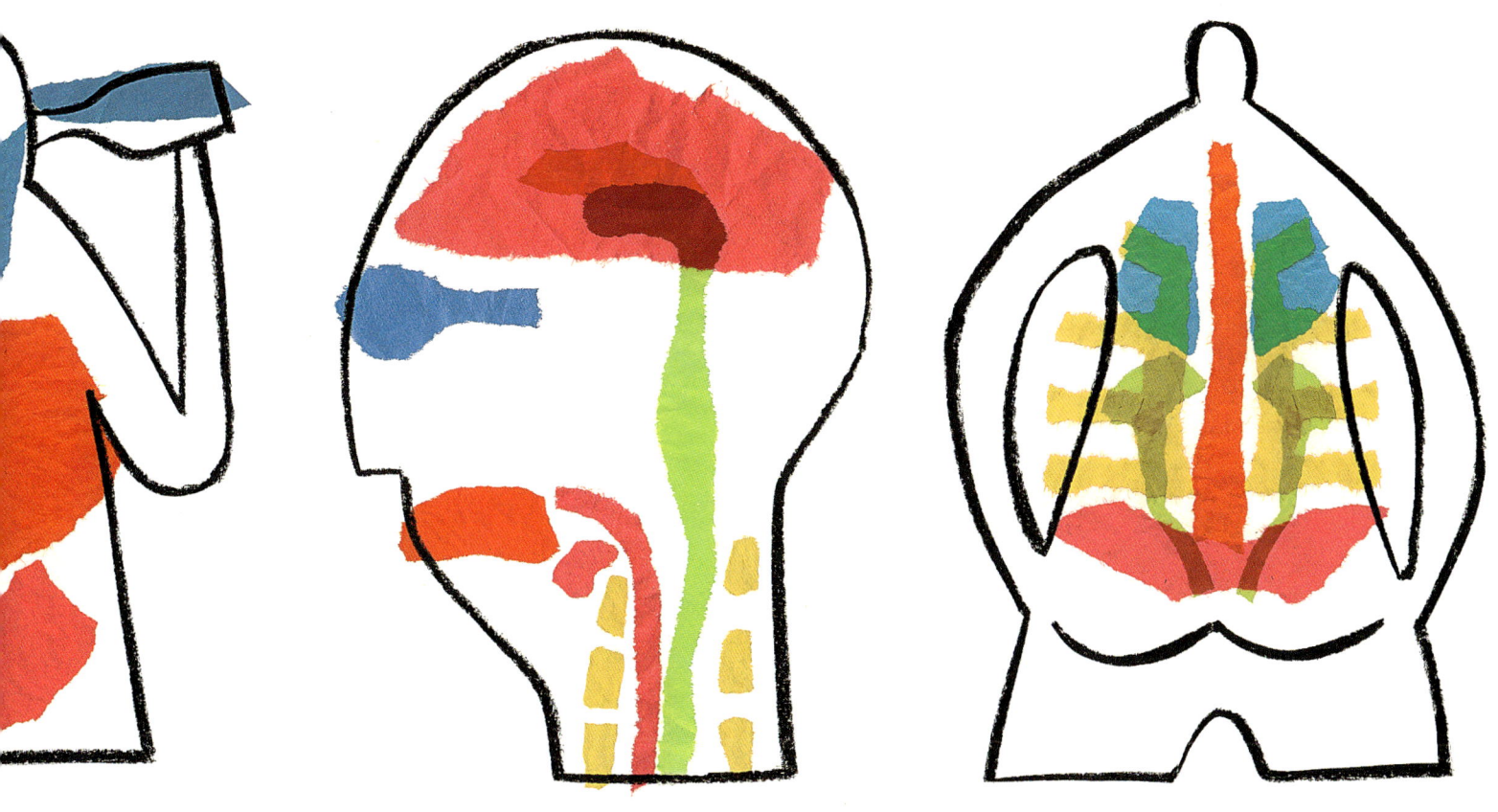

PYOTR ZHILICHKIN
Russia

Title of Work
The Feathers

Technique
Watercolour

Captions
· *Mikado Pheasant Feather*
· *Little Egret Feather*
· *Mikado Pheasant*

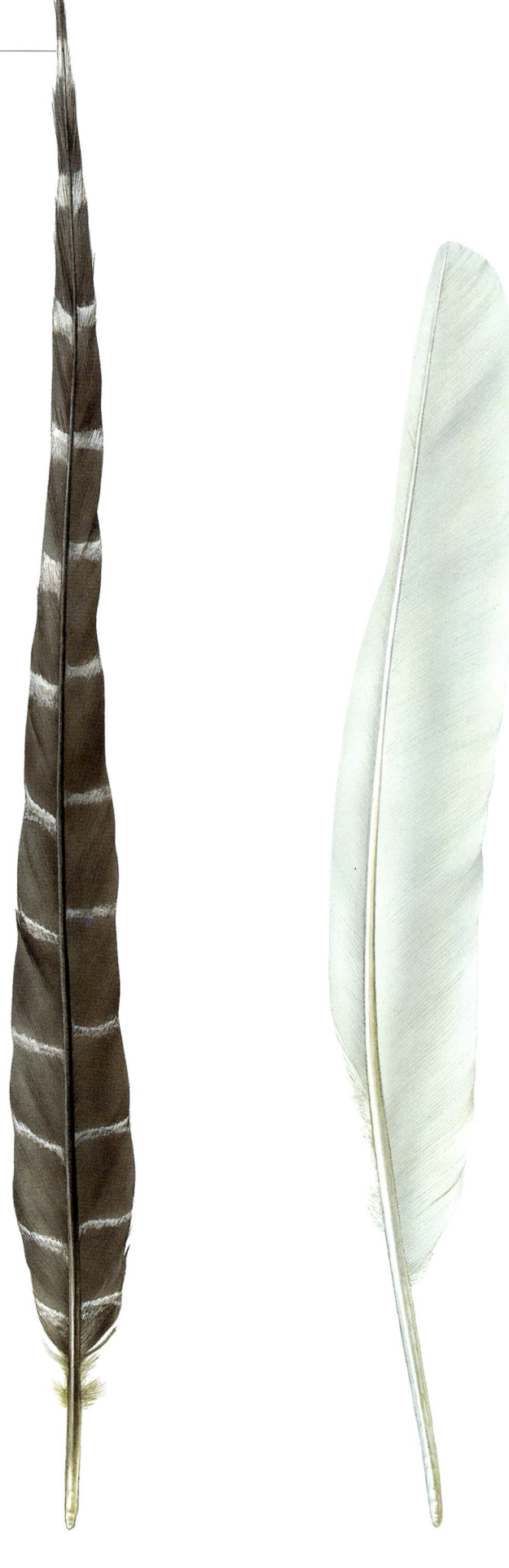

Looking ahead to the **2008 ILLUSTRATORS EXHIBITION**

The FICTION and NON FICTION Illustrators Exhibition is a unique event offering young illustrators an opportunity to gain valuable exposure, and providing publishers with an extremely useful service of the very highest quality. The illustrations submitted are examined and selected by an international panel of publishers and art college teachers. We wish to extend a special invitation to:

ILLUSTRATORS, both professionals and newcomers, to submit their unpublished works or illustrations published in the last two years

ART COLLEGES AND SCHOOLS OF ILLUSTRATION, to submit their student's works and projects

PUBLISHERS, to present their most prestigious illustrators and artists at this top-level venue.

The deadline for the submission of your original artwork is **19 OCTOBER 2007** both for **FICTION** and **NON FICTION**

Illustrators Exhibition/Bologna 31 March – 3 April 2008

Copyright © 2007
Bologna Children's Book Fair
Piazza Costituzione 6
40128 Bologna, Italy

Published in Italy by:
BolognaFiereWeb S.r.l.
Via Maserati, 20
40128 Bologna, Italy
Tel. +39 051 4158167
Fax +39 051 4154887
e-mail: info@bolognafiereweb.it

Copublished with
minedition rights & licensing ag
Mühlebachstrasse 82
CH-8034 Zürich
Switzerland
Phone +41 1 380 5740
www.minedition.com

Coproduced with
Michael Neugebauer Publishing Ltd
Unit 808, Metro Centre II
21 Lam Hing Street
Kowloon Bay
Hong Kong
Tel. +852 2147 0303
Fax +852 2147 0308
www.minedition.com

Distributions:

Austria / Germany / Switzerland:
minedition
Michael Neugebauer Edition GmbH
Am Gerstenfeld 6
D-22941 Bargteheide
Tel.: 49(0)4532/268700
Fax: 49(0)4532/ 268701
www.minedition.com
info@minedition.de
ISBN 978-3-86566-702-1

France:
minedition France
c/o SOFEDIS
11, rue Soufflot
F-75005 Paris
Tel. +33 1 53 10 25 25
Fax +33 1 53 10 25 26

Netherland
De Vier Windstreken
Ampèrelaan 3
2289 CD Rijswijk
Tel. 070-4131191
www.vierwindstreken.com

USA:
minedition published by
Penguing Young Readers Group
345 Hudson Street
New York, NY 10014
www.penguin.com
www.minedition.com
ISBN 978-0-698-40061-0

Asia:
Michael Neugebauer Publishing Ltd
Unit 808, Metro Centre II
21 Lam Hing Street
Kowloon Bay
Hong Kong
Tel. +852 2147 0303
Fax +852 2147 0308
www.minedition.com

Graphic Designer:
G.Lanzi, Bologna

Lithographed film
Fotoriproduzioni
Ermanno.Beverari,
Verona, Italy

Printer, supervisor:
minedition
Michael Neugebauer
Publishing Ltd. Hong Kong

For information:

Illustrators Exhibition
Piazza Costituzione 6
40128 Bologna (Italy)
Tel. +39 051 282111
Fax +39 051 6374011
e-mail:
illustratori@bolognafiere.it

BolognaFiere S.p.a.
assumes no responsibility
for any omission, incorrect
information and
description, oversight or
printing error in respect of
the illustrators' names
and curricula vitae.

All rights reserved
Printed in Hong Kong

ILLUSTRATORS

BIOGRAPHIES

Hassan Amekan

Address
c/o Kanoon - International Affairs Institute for the Intellectual Development of Children and Young Adults
Fatemi Av., Hejab Street
141456 Tehran – Iran
Tel. +98 21 889 673 92
Fax. +98 21 882 11 21
e-mail: hassan.amekan@gmail.com

Place and Date of Birth
Guilan, Iran, 1979

Published Titles
Run and Run, Cheesta
Ferdousi's Shahnameh, Cheesta
The Magical Drop, Shinseken Ldt., Japan
Wall in the my Heart, Tavakol
Donkey was Not Donkey, Madreseh

Technique
Mixed

Yuko Aoki

Address
Via Calligherie, 13
48018 Faenza, Italy
Tel. +39 338 9102096
e-mail: aoiuo@hotmail.com

Place and Date of Birth
Nara, Japan, 13 February 1980

Technique
Etching

▲ **UNPUBLISHED** ▲

Keiko Arakawa

Address
1-6-57 Toyota machi Toyama City
931-8313 Toyama, Japan
Tel. +81 076.443 12 66
Fax. +81 076.443 12 66
e-mail: keikok_a@d6.dion.ne.jp

Place and Date of Birth
Toyama, Japan, 7 May 1971

Technique
Etching

▲ **UNPUBLISHED** ▲

Giovanni Ballestra

Address
Via Borgo San Pietro, 8
40126 Bologna, Italy
Tel. +39 051 22 52 21

Place and Date of Birth
Forlì, Italy, 11 October 1962

Technique
Watercolor

▲ U N P U B L I S H E D ▲

Behnoush Behnzadi Azad

Address
No. 3, Shahin Alley, Sepah Street, Sepah Sq.
16117 Tehran, Iran
Tel. +98 21 776 36 839
Fax. +98 21 776 36 839
e-mail: behnoushbehzadi@gmail.com

Place and Date of Birth
Tehran, Iran, 21 September 1982

Technique
Mixed

▲ U N P U B L I S H E D ▲

Francesca Bolis

Address
Via Statale, 27/E
23881 Airuno, Italy
Tel. +39 334 132 77 49
e-mail: frabolis@hotmail.com

Place and Date of Birth
Lecco, Italy, 28 September 1982

Technique
Acrylic, collage

▲ U N P U B L I S H E D ▲

p. 174   *p. 32*   *p. 34*

Irène Bonacina

Address
4, Quai au Sable
67000 Strasbourg, France
Tel. +33 06 788 95 704
e-mail: irenebonaci@hotmail.com

Place and Date of Birth
Paris, France, 7 February 1984

Art School Attended
ESAD - Ecole Supérieure des Arts Décoratifs de Strasbourg

School Director
Katia Baudin Reneau

Co-ordinator
Guillaume Dégé

Technique
Black Ink

▲ U N P U B L I S H E D ▲

Jennifer Bongibault

Address
98, Rue Pelleport
75020 Paris
Tel. +33 06 23631310
e-mail: jenniferbongibault@yahoo.fr

Place and Date of Birth
Paris, France 8 April 1982

Art School Attended
ENSAD - Ecole Nationale Supérieure des Arts Décoratifs

School Director
Patrick Raynaud

Co-ordinator
Denis Perus

Technique
Serigraph, Ink

▲ U N P U B L I S H E D ▲

Ali Boozari

Address
c/o Shabaviz Publishing Co.
No.2, Nouri Alley, Jomhouri Eslami Ave.,
Between Golshan St. and Bastan St.
13186 – 45163 Tehran, Iran
Tel. +98 21 664 23 995
Fax. +98 21 6642 7858
e-mail: shabaviz@shabaviz.com

Place and Date of Birth
Tehran, Iran 1977

Published Titles
Parinaz or Nazpari, Shabaviz, Tehran
Capped Bear and Capless, Shabaviz, Tehran
Redskirt, Shabaviz, Tehran
The Tailless Fox, Shabaviz, Tehran
The Land of Water – lilies, Shabaviz, Tehran

Technique
Mixed

p. 176   *p. 36*   *p. 38*

Mathilde Bourgon

Address
342, Rue des Pyrénées
75020 Paris, France
Tel. +33 06 03861260
e-mail: mathilde.bourgon@ensad.fr

Place and Date of Birth
Besançon, France, 25 September 1985

Art School Attended
ENSAD - Ecole Nationale Supérieure des Arts Décoratifs

School Director
Patrick Raynaud

Co-ordinator
Denis Perus

Technique
Serigraph

▲ U N P U B L I S H E D ▲

p. 40

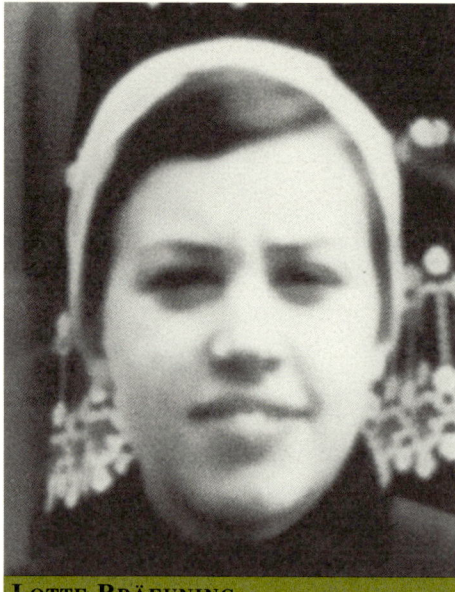

Lotte Bräeuning

Address
Osterbrook, 22
20537 Hamburg, Germany
Tel. +49 040 21059847
e-mail: lotte.braeuning@gmx.de

Place and Date of Birth
Stuttgart, Germany 18 January 1982

Art School Attended
HAW - Hamburg University of Applied Sciences

School Director
Dorothea Wenzel

Co-ordinator
Bernd Mölch-Tassel

Technique
Pencil, acrylic

▲ U N P U B L I S H E D ▲

p. 42

Guglielmo Calciolari

Address
Piazza F. Cavallotti, 1
46100 Mantova, Italy
Tel. +39 0376 322 010
e-mail: calcio14@alice.it

Place and Date of Birth
Mantova, Italy, 5 August 1980

Technique
Ink

▲ U N P U B L I S H E D ▲

p. 178

Claudia Carls

Address
Mühlendamm, 51
22087 Hamburg, Germany
Tel. +49 040 239 386 68
e-mail: claudia.carls@gmx.de

Place and Date of Birth
Hamburg, Germany, 5 October 1978

Art School Attended
HAW – Hamburg University of Applied Sciences

School Director
Dorothea Wenzel

Co-ordinator
Bernd Mölch-Tassel

Technique
Photo of small clay-sculpture, digitally combined with computer-coloured pencil drawing

▲ U N P U B L I S H E D ▲

p. 44

André Carvalho

Address
Estrada da Azenha, 74
3800-086 Alagoas-Santa Joana
Aveiro, Portugal
Tel. +351 964 33 05 56
e-mail: andre@boxdesign.info

Place and Date of Birth
Aveiro, Portugal, 13 September 1979

Art School Attended
Design na Universidade de Aveiro – Portugal

Published Titles
Meia Bola, Edições Éterogémeas, Porto

Technique
Acrylic, stencil

p. 46

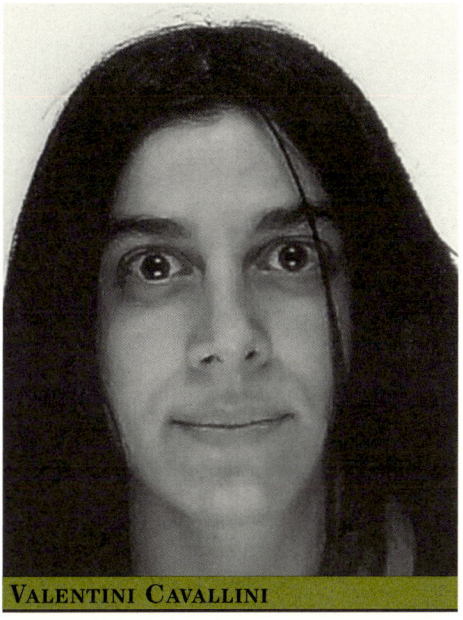

Valentini Cavallini

Address
68, Upper Cheltenham Place
BS6 5HR Bristol, Great Britain
Tel. +44 11 79542410
e-mail: valentinas.world@gmail.com

Place and Date of Birth
Milano, Italy, 26 May 1975

Art School Attended
Chelsea College of Art and Design

Technique
Collage, digital

▲ U N P U B L I S H E D ▲

p. 48

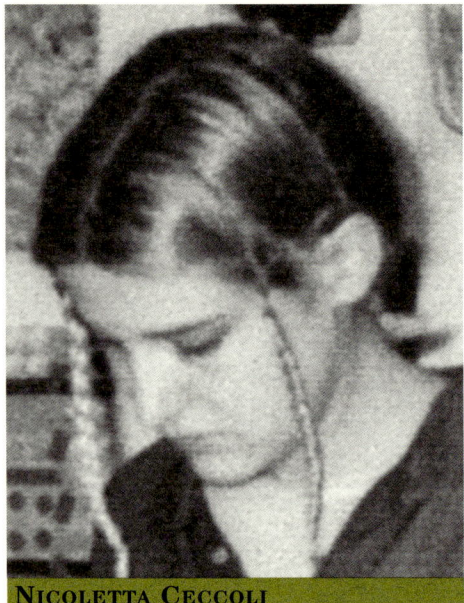

Nicoletta Ceccoli

Address
Via 28 luglio, 184
47893 Borgo Maggiore, RSM
Tel. +39 0549 907728
e-mail: nceccoli@omniway.sm

Place and Date of Birth
R. di San Marino, 17 March 1973

Published Titles
Nuvolando, Edizioni Arka, Milano
Foresta radice Labirinto, Mondadori, Verona
Pinocchio, Mondadori, Verona
Fiabe di Perrault, Mondatori, Verona
A immagine e somiglianza, Fatatrac, Firenze
Talpa lumaca pesciolino, Fatatrac, Firenze
An Island in the Sun, Barefoot Books, UK
The Princess and the White Bear King, Barefoot Books, UK
The Faery's Gift, Barefoot Books, UK
Little Red Hiding Hood, Barefoot Books, UK
The Barefoot Books of Faery Tales, Barefoot Books, UK
Firefighters in the Dark, Houghton Mifflin, Boston
Village of Basketeers, Houghton Mifflin, Boston
Oscar and the Mooncats, Houghton Mifflin, Boston
Girl in the Castle, Random House, USA

Technique
Acrylics, Photoshop

p. 50

Maja Celija

Address
Via Domenico Mazza, 54
61100 Pesaro, Italy
Tel. +39 0721 371854
e-mail: stomach@inwind.it

Place and Date of Birth
Maribor, Slovenia, 10 March 1977

Published Titles
Happy Prince, Woong-jin, Corea del Sud
Il piccolo e il gigante feroce, Carthusia, Milano
Filastrocca acqua e sapone per bambini con i piedi sporchi, Topipittori, Milano
Chiuso per ferie, Topipittori, Milano
Ventun fiabe bruttebelle, Fatatrac, Firenze
Mille et un contes (Histoires de bons et mauvais génies), Editions Milan
Mille et un contes (Histoires de filous et de brigands), Editions Milan
Mille et un contes (Histoires de sirènes et autres créatures fabuleuses), Editions Milan
Contes de monsieur chat, Editions Milan
Filastrocca delle mani, Topipittori, Milano

Technique
Acrylics on paper

p. 52

Isabelle Chattelard

Address
La forge de Prasset
73590 Flumet, France
Tel. +33 47 9318189
e-mail: courrier@isabellechatellard.fr

Place and Date of Birth
Sallanches, France 24 January 1970

Published Titles
Ermeline et sa machine, Editions du Rouergue
Olivia à Paris, Pastel/ Ecole des Loisirs
Les Chocottes, Editions du Rouergue
Le corbeau de paradis, Pastel/ Ecole des Loisirs
Le Noël de maître Belloni, Flammarion
Pied D'Or, Pastel/Ecole del Loisirs
Le Navet, L'Ecole des loisirs
Le rat de ville et le rat des champs, Nathan
Figaro's Wedding, Grimm Press
Le petit tour, Autrement
Pantin la Pirouette, Dessin Animé
La nuit du Melimos, Flammarion
A pas de velours, Didier
Les Dames, Didier Jeunesse
Ma couverture et moi, Casterman
La galette des trois, Flammarion
Le petit poucet, Didier
Neuf contes tout neufs de fées et de princesses, Nathan
Jeux de piste, Bilboquet/Art à la page
La complainte du phoque en Alaska, Didier
Conte d'Ivachka, Nathan
Pantin la pirouette, Albin Michel
Les Oies sauvages, Bilboquet
Sur le fil, Nathan
Les Histoires d'amour ne sont pas toujours simples, Tourbillon
Au fils des flots, Didier
La piste aux Etoiles, Bilboquet
L'ours de Noël, Bilboquet
Le petit chapeaux rond rouge et le grand lougoudou

Technique

p. 54

Julia Chausson

Address
128, Rue Ordener
75018 Paris, France
Tel. +33 01 44 85 00 50
e-mail: juliachausson@hotmail.com

Place and Date of Birth
Paris, France, 12 January 1977

Published Titles
Le grand secret de Tim, Grasset, Paris
Le grand livre des princesses, Albin Michel, Paris
Le petit Marco et les maisons du monde, Mitik, Lyon
Etrangère au paradis, Grasset, Paris
Mon poemier, Mango, Paris

Technique
Mixed

p. 56

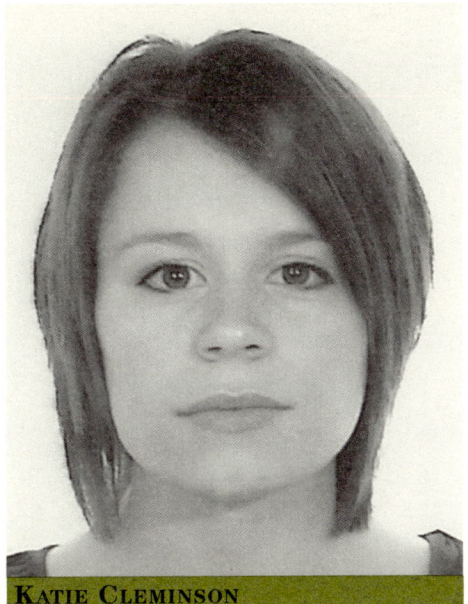

Katie Cleminson

Address
Roseberry, Red Shute Hill
RG18 9QW, Newbury
Great Britain
Tel. +44 0774 88 75 882
e-mail: kt_cleminson@hotmail.com

Place and Date of Birth
Berkshire, 7 June, 1984

Art School Attended
Art Wales School of Art and Design

School Director
Sion Hughes

Co-ordinator
Sue Thornton

Technique
Mixed media

▲ UNPUBLISHED ▲

p. 58

Patrizia Donaera

Address
Via XX Settembre, 5/7
17100 Savona, Italy
Tel. +39 0198485018
e-mail: patrizia@patriziadonaera.it

Place and Date of Birth
Cuneo, Italy 13 April 1964

Published Titles
1,2,3...indovina chi è?, De agostini Ragazzi, Milano
Mamme e bebè dimmi chi è?, De agostini Ragazzi, Milano
Petits écureuils, Les livres du Dragon d'Or, Paris
Petits canards, Les livres du Dragon d'Or, Paris
Le corbeau et le renard et autres fables, Nathan, Paris
Serpolet Cornillon, lapin de garenne, Nathan, Paris
Grignotte l'écureuil, Nathan, Paris
Guide du jeune Robinson à la campagne, Nathan, Paris
Petit Mega des animaux, Nathan, Paris
Where do Babies Come from?, Dorling Kindersley Children's Book, London
Tadpoles and Frogs, Usborne, London
Night Animals, Usborne, London
Dogs, Usborne, London
Cats, Usborne, London
Mar Ligure, l'uomo e il mare, Ergaedizioni, Genova
A Little Book of Sheeds, Pinwheel, London
A Little Book of Eggs, Pinwheel, London

Technique
Watercolor

p. 180

Biagio Forgione

Address
Via Osasco, 101
10141 Torino, Italy
Tel. +39 338 1808172
e-mail: mail@biagioforgione.com

Place and Date of Birth
Gesualdo, Italy, 1 September 1968

Art School Attended
Primo Liceo Artistico di Torino

Published Titles
Flautissimo, Rugginenti
Piemonte Parchi, Febbraio 1997

Technique
Acrylic on paper

p. 60

Marianna Fulvi

Address
Via Flaminia, 153
61041 Acqualagna (PU) – Italy
Tel. +39 339 6638495
e-mail: mari_io@virgilio.it

Place and Date of Birth
Fossombrone, Italy, 21 November 1983

Art School Attended
Istituto Europeo di Design di Milano

Technique
Digital

▲ U N P U B L I S H E D ▲

p. 62

François Garnier

Address
29, rue Victor Bosch
69100 Villeurbanne, France
Tel. +33 06 1684 2447
e-mail: art008@wanadoo.fr

Place and Date of Birth
Feurs, France 8 May 1983

Art School Attended
ENBA - Ecole Nationale Des Beaux Arts de Lyon

School Director
Yves Robert

Co-ordinator
Jean Claverie

Technique
Mixed

▲ U N P U B L I S H E D ▲

p. 182

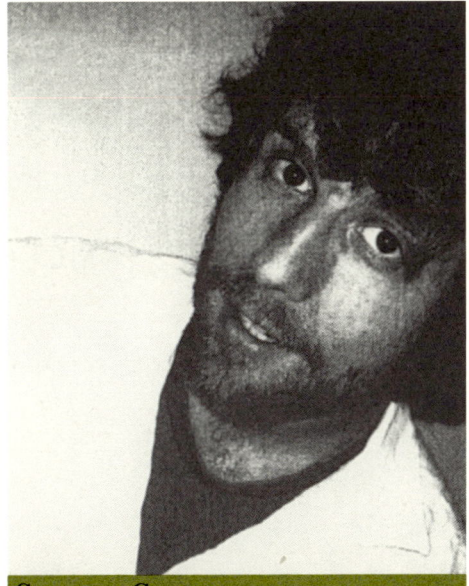

Staffan Gnosspelius

Address
72, Arlingford Road
SW2 2TA London, Great Britain
Tel. +44 7984969112
e-mail: staffan@gnosspelius.com

Place and Date of Birth
Lund, Sweden 24 May 1976

Published Titles
The Snot Book, Ratatosk Publishing, London

Technique
Silk-screen Prints

p. 64

Roberta Gorni

Address
Via San Pio X, 42
31046 Oderzo (TV), Italy
Tel. +39 338 9938 006
e-mail: robygorni@yahoo.it

Place and Date of Birth
Oderzo, Italy 31 January 1979

Art School Attended
Istituto Universitario di Venezia

Published Titles
Bruna non vuole fare il bagno, Fatatrac, Firenze
Elia non vuole andare a letto, Fatatrac, Firenze
Gino non vuole mangiare la minestra, Fatatrac, Firenze
Flora non vuole vestirsi, Fatatrac, Firenze

Technique
Acrylic, pencils, pastels

p. 66

Cédric Guarneri

Address
6, petite rue Pasteur
69100 Villeurbanne, France
Tel. +33 0871083442
e-mail: zedrik@free.fr

Place and Date of Birth
Lyon, France 1 July 1983

Art School Attended
Ecole Emile Cohl

School Director
Philippe Rivière

Co-ordinator
Frédéric Mansot

Technique
Acrylic, linocut

▲ UNPUBLISHED ▲

p. 184

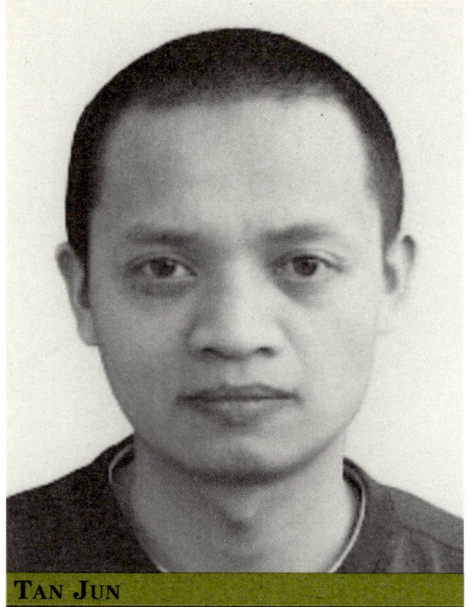

Tan Jun

Address
Room 101, N° 10, YongQing
Residential Quarter 1, BaoShan District
200940 Shangai, China
Tel. +86 10 81632565
e-mail: tanjun_0086@yahoo.com.cn

Place and Date of Birth
XiangTan, China, 22 October 1973

Technique
Charcoal, Acrylic, Tea, Papers, Ink

▲ U N P U B L I S H E D ▲

Franz Kainz

Address
Novaragasse, 55/11
1020 Vienna, Austria
Tel. +43 196 80 813
e-mail: franz-k.1@gmx.net

Place and Date of Birth
Vienna, Austria 13 March 1964

Technique
Ink, watercolor

▲ U N P U B L I S H E D ▲

Saori Kamino

Address
705-1 Dai 2 Nishikata Kuwana-shi
511-0864 Mie-ken, Japan
Tel. +81 52 764 1522
e-mail: takapei_com@yahoo.co.jp

Place and Date of Birth
Mie, Japan, 5 April 1975

Art School Attended
Nakagawa Art School of Picture Books

School Director
Takako Nakagawa

Technique
Acrylic

▲ U N P U B L I S H E D ▲

p. 68   *p. 70*   *p. 72*

Tibor Kárpáti

Address
31, Vaskapu
6729 Szeged, Hungary
Tel. +36 30 282 9868
e-mail: karpatitibor@yahoo.com

Place and Date of Birth
Gyula, Hungary 17 May 1978

Published Titles
Piroska és a farkas, Csimota, Budapest

Technique
Computer

Dorte Karrebæk

Address
Enchinent 4C
03710 Calpe, Spagna
Tel. +34 965837595
e-mail: dortekarrebaek@mail-onlinedk

Place and Date of Birth
Denmark, 19 July 1946

Published Titles
DE TRE NR. II, da Carlo Blev midt over af en stor, stor hund, Dansklærerforeningen Forlag

Technique
Watercolor, Ink

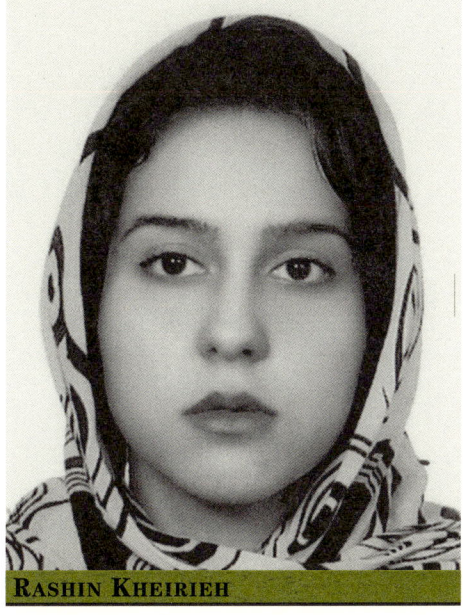
Rashin Kheirieh

Address
c/o Kanoon - International Affairs Institute for the Intellectual Development of Children and Young Adults
Fatemi Av., Hejab Street
141456 Tehran – Iran
Tel. +98 21 889 673 92
Fax. +98 21 882 11 21
e-mail: kanoon@jamejam.net

Place and Date of Birth
Khoramshahr, Iran 26 September 1979

Art School Attended
Art University of Tehran

Published Titles
The White Forest, Grandir, France
The Golden Axe, Isabel, France
The Famous Smile, Katha, India
Evangelist Prays for Children, Bayard, France
The Foxy Tailor, France
Moon Titi, Cap Titi, Center for Intellectual Promotion of Children and Young Adults, Tehran, Iran
The Red Bus, Madreseh Pub., Tehran, Iran

Technique
Linoleum

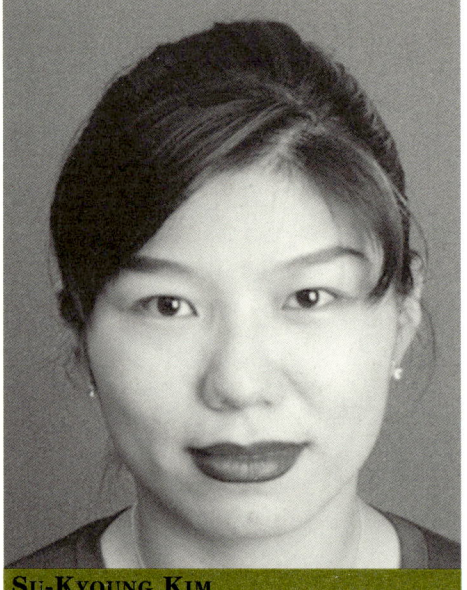

Su-Kyoung Kim

Address
791 1328 Mia 2-dong,
Gangbuk-gu 142-102
Seoul, Republic of Korea
Tel. +82 2 945 2284
Fax. +82 2 3142 1180
e-mail: album1013@hanmail.net

Place and Date of Birth
Seoul, Republic of Korea, 8 November 1972

Art School Attended
Kingston University, U.K.

Published Titles
Lucky Pig at the Street Corner, Darim Publishing Co.

Technique
Collage on tracing paper

p. 80

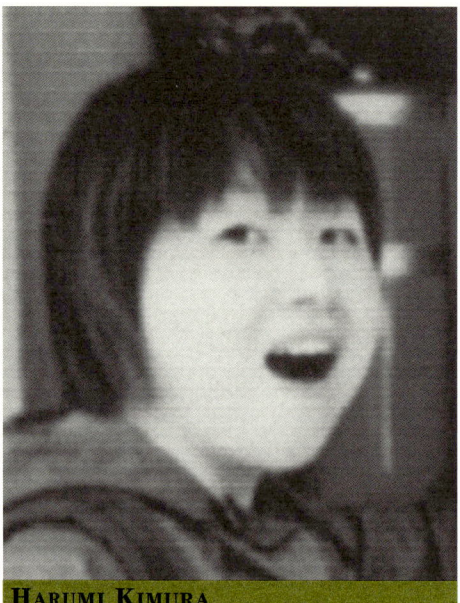

Harumi Kimura

Address
1 Kaminoura Toride-shi
300-1524 Ibraki, Japan
Tel. +81 29 78 26171
e-mail: info@kimuraharumi.jp

Place and Date of Birth
Ibraki, Japan 20 April 1977

Technique
Mixed

▲ U N P U B L I S H E D ▲

p. 82

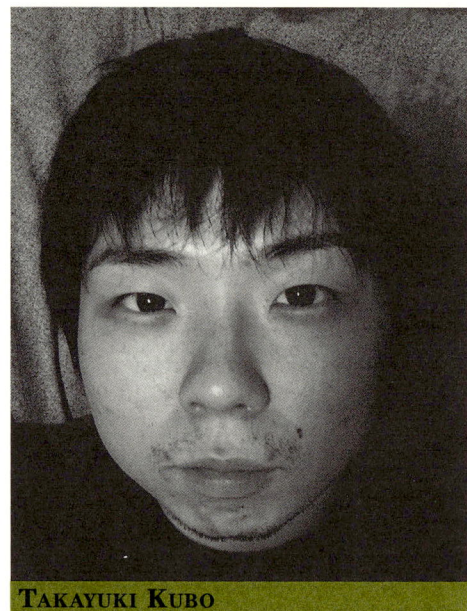

Takayuki Kubo

Address
205, Mukaiumeso, Mukaiumecho,
Kamigano, Kitaku, Kyotoshi
603 8086 Kyoto, Japan
Tel. +81 07424 66 152
e-mail: kansyoku-no-nai-nukumori@r9.dion.ne.jp

Place and Date of Birth
Nara, Japan 28 May 1981

Technique
Mezzotint

▲ U N P U B L I S H E D ▲

p. 84

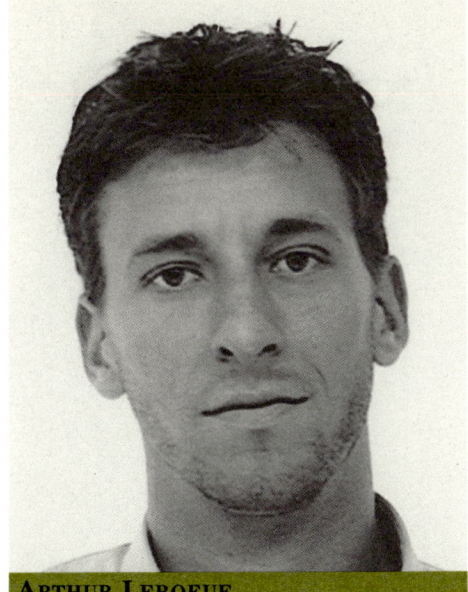

Arthur Leboeuf

Address
222, avenue Félix Faure
69003 Lyon, France
Tel. +33 06 79 54 1947
e-mail: albeef@free.fr

Place and Date of Birth
Schiltigheim, France 18 May 1978

Art School Attended
Ecole Emile Cohl

School Director
Philippe Rivière

Co-ordinator
Frédéric Mansot

Technique
Gouache

▲ U N P U B L I S H E D ▲

Alessandro Lecis

Address
Res. Fontana MI 2
20090 Segrate (MI), Italy
Tel. +39 340 6672548
e-mail: el.graf@tiscali.it

Place and Date of Birth
Milano, Italy 13 November 1975

Published Titles
Ti prendo ti prendo, Orecchio Acerbo, Roma

Technique
Collage, acrylic, computer graphic

Teresa Lima

Address
Rua Aristides de Sousa Mendes N° 2-8-F.te
1600-413 Lisboa, Portugal
Tel. +351 210141346
e-mail: teresalimagoncalves@clix.pt

Place and Date of Birth
Lisboa, Portugal 14 March 1962

Published Titles
Historias de Animais de Rudyard Kipling, Ambar Editor, Porto
A Noite dos Animais Inventados, Presença, Lisboa
Se os Bichos se vestissem como Gente, Civilização, Porto
A Cavalo no tempo, Civilização, Porto
Alice no Pais das Maravilhas, Civilização, Porto
António e o Principezinho, Ambar, Porto
Á cor das Vogais, Civilização, Porto

Technique
Mixed

Davide Longaretti / Mayuko Tazumi

Address
Viale Ranzoni, 3
20149 Milano, Italy
Tel. +39 02 403 95 99
e-mail: davide.longaretti@fastwebnet.it

Place and Date of Birth
Davide Longaretti
Verbania, Italy 27 September 1979

Mayuko Tazumi
Osaka, Japan

Technique
Mixed (plasticine, graphic computer)

▲ U N P U B L I S H E D ▲

p. 92

Golnaz Mahmoodi

Address
c/o Kanoon - International Affairs
Institute for the Intellectual
Development of Children and Young
Adults
Fatemi Av., Hejab Street
141456 Tehran – Iran
Tel. +98 21 889 673 92
Fax. +98 21 888 211 21
e-mail: kanoon@jamejam.net

Place and Date of Birth
Tehran, 1983

Technique
Mixed

▲ U N P U B L I S H E D ▲

p. 94

Gabriella Makhult

Address
Avar utca, 8
2092 Budakeszi, Hungary
Tel. +36 70 5211264
e-mail: gaabica@yahoo.co.uk

Place and Date of Birth
Budapest, Hungary 8 May 1981

Published Titles
Török Sophie èletregènye, Èghajlat, Budapest
Török Sophie Kiadatlan Szerelmes versei, Èghajlat, Budapest
Magazine "Szegletjö", Szederkènyi, Budapest
Magazine "Csangò tukor", Budapest
Saint Francesco and the Wolf, Own publishing, Budapest

Technique
Linocut, Ink-paint

p. 96

Gémeo Luís Mendonça

Address
Rua do Rosário, 223
4050-524 Porto, Portugal
Tel. +351 22 338 95 23
Fax. +351 22 338 95 22
e-mail: luismendonca@netcabo.pt

Place and Date of Birth
Mozambique, 13 March 1965

Published Titles
O Quê Que Quem, Edições Éterogémeas, Porto
Sssschlep, Edições Éterogémeas, Porto
O Piano de Cauda, Edições Éterogémeas, Porto
Palavra que Voa, Caminho, Lisboa
O Sam e o Som, Caminho, Lisboa

Technique
Craft Paper cutting

p. 98

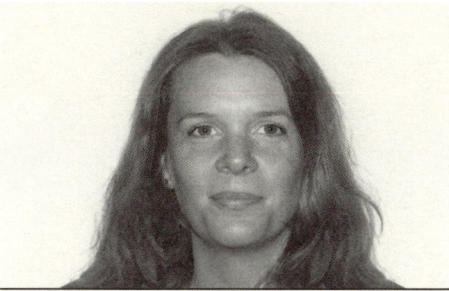

Anne Misfeld / Jørgen Stamp

Address
Flintebakken, 190
8240 Risskov, Denmark
Tel. +45 86121018
e-mail: jstamp@mail.dk

Place and Date of Birth
Anne Misfeld
Århus, Denmark 9 August 1971

Jørgen Stamp
Århus, Denmark 27 October 1969

Published Titles
'Flyv' Forlaget Carlsen, Copenhagen
'Kør', Forlaget Carlsen, Copenhagen

Technique
Collage

p. 100

Taro Miura

Address
3-21-5-303, Sendagaya, Shibuya-ku
151-0051 Tokyo, Japan
Tel. +81 3 5772 8515
Fax. +81 3 5772 8516
e-mail: info@taromiura.com

Place and Date of Birth
Nishio, Japan 28 November 1968

Published Titles
Je suis…, La Joie de lire, Switzerland
Ton, Edizioni Corraini, Mantova
Kuttuita, Kogumasya, Japan
Arnesi/Tools, Edizioni Corraini, Mantova
Bokuwamaru, Bronze Publishing Inc., Japan
Bokuwasankaku, Bronze Publishing Inc., Japan
Des Jours Pas Comme Les Autres, La Joie De Lire, Switzerland
Tokio, Media Vaca, Spain
Naranda, Koguamasya, Japan
Lavori in Corso, Edizioni Corraini, Mantova

Technique
Computer Graphics

p. 186

STEFANO MORRI

Address
Via Galileo Galilei, 15
47900 Rimini, Italy
Tel. +39 0549 907728
e-mail: stefanomorri@yahoo.it

Place and Date of Birth
Rimini, Italy 21 June 1973

Published Titles
Cappuccetto Rosso, Edizioni Arka, Milano

Technique
Mixed, Computer Graphic

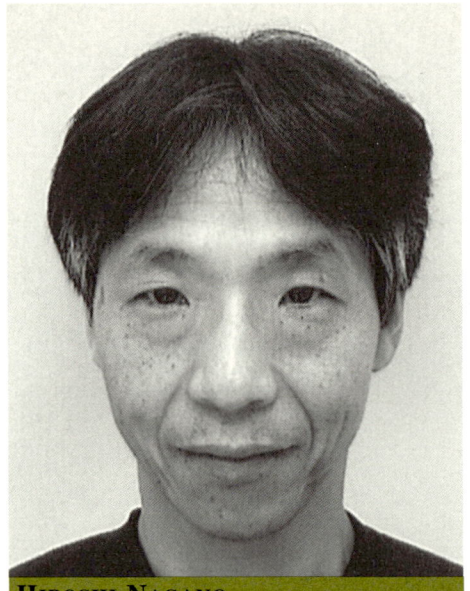

HIROSHI NAGANO

Address
3-122-1 Nyukai-cho Kakamigahar-city
504-0833 Gifu, Japan
Tel. +81 058 389 1268
Fax. +81 058 389 1268
e-mail: nagano111jp@yahoo.co.jp

Place and Date of Birth
Gifu, Japan 22 September 1954

Technique
Watercolor

▲ U N P U B L I S H E D ▲

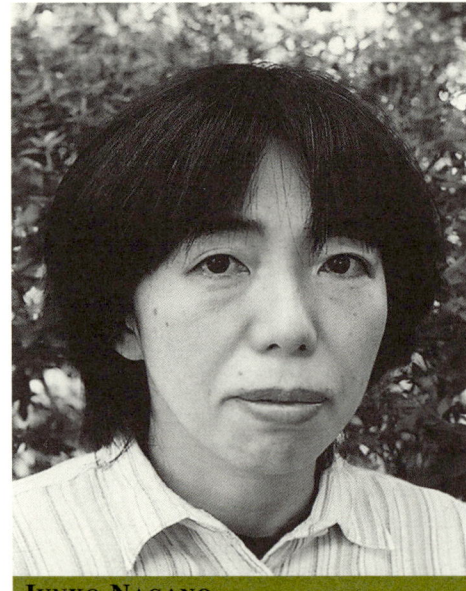

JUNKO NAGANO

Address
60-3 Tukunawa-machi, Takasaki-city
370-0075 Gunma, Japan
Tel. +81 027 361 3656
Fax. +81 027 361 3656

Place and Date of Birth
Gunma, Japan 11 April 1966

Published Titles
Boku to Hikati to Entei de, Tokuma Shoten publishing Co. Ltd, Tokyo

Technique
Etching

Ely Nakayama

Address
Via Trento, 1/B
20060 Cassina de' Pecchi (MI), Italy
Tel. +39 02 95343165
Fax. +39 02 50321640
e-mail: ely.nakayama@yahoo.it

Place and Date of Birth
Maringà, Brazil 14 March 1958

Technique
Acrylic on paper

▲ U N P U B L I S H E D ▲

p. 108

Nanni Elisa

Address
Via I Maggio, 20
61016 Pennabilli (PU), Italy
Tel. +39 380 3913812
e-mail: lisanannina@yahoo.it

Place and Date of Birth
Novafeltria (PU), Italy 30 June 1983

Art School Attended
ISIA Urbino

School Director
Franco Mariani

Co-ordinator
Sandro Natalini

Technique
Acrylic, pastels

p. 110

Franziska Neubert

Address
Leibnizstrasse, 13
04105 Leipzig, Germany
Tel. +49 341 9 83 24 52
e-mail: franziska.neubert@web.de

Place and Date of Birth
Leipzig, Germany 15 June 1977

Art School Attended
Hochschule für Grafik und Buchkunst, Leipzig

School Director
Joachim Brohm

Co-ordinator
Thomas Mattheus Müller

Published Titles
Le Grand Frère, La Joie de lire, Switzerland

Technique
Offset original

p. 202

Yoshiko Noda

Address
2-32-1 Tarumi Suita-city
564-0062 Osaka, Japan
Tel. +81 6 6386 2663
Fax. +81 6 6386 2663
e-mail: yosika21@hotmail.com

Place and Date of Birth
Osaka, Japan 31 December 1980

Published Titles
Giornale Italia in Arte Fiera, Maurizio Corraini S.r.l., Mantova

Technique
Pen and Ink

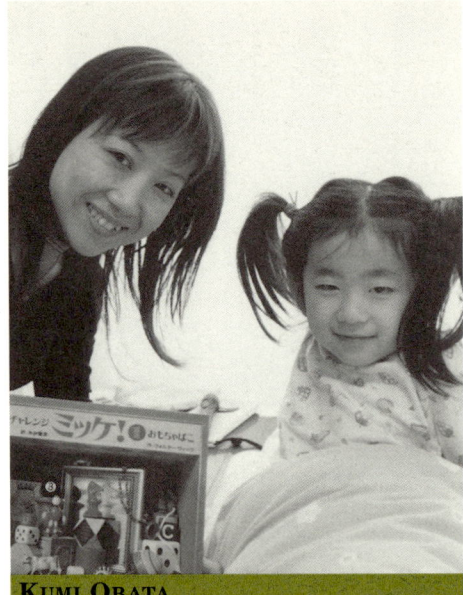

Kumi Obata

Address
2-37-1 Minamikarasuyama 203,
Setagaya-ku
157-0062 Tokyo, Japan
Tel. +81 3 5313 3846
Fax. +81 3 5313 3846
e-mail: pocot@pd6.so-net.ne.jp

Place and Date of Birth
Kanagawa, Japan 4 February 1966

Technique
Etching

▲ U N P U B L I S H E D ▲

Andrea Offerman

Address
Engelswisch, 22
23552 Lübeck, Germany
Tel. +49 451 370 4951
e-mail: andreaofferman@gmail.com

Place and Date of Birth
Köln, Germany 28 June 1980

Art School Attended
Art Center College of Design,
Pasadena, CA

Technique
Pen and Ink, oil, digital

▲ U N P U B L I S H E D ▲

p. 114   *p. 116*   *p. 118*

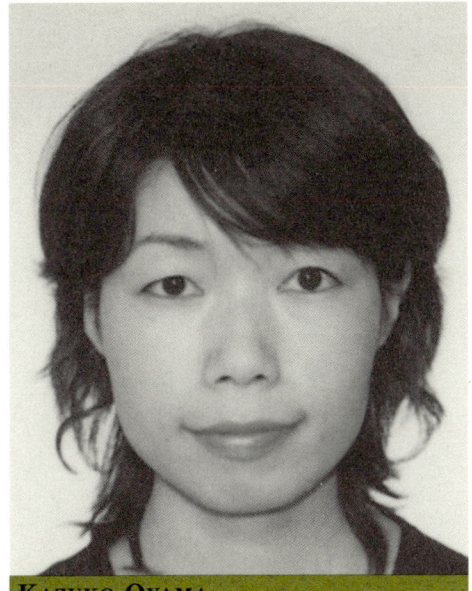

Kazuko Oyama

Address
Tokiwadai 6-11-4, Toyonocho,
563-0102 Toyonogun, Osaka, Japan
Tel. +81 072 738 1372
Fax. +81 072 738 1372
e-mail: kazu-314@zeus.eonet.ne.jp

Place and Date of Birth
Osaka, Japan 14 March 1972

Technique
Computer Graphic

▲ U N P U B L I S H E D ▲

p. 120

Gabriel Pacheco

Address
Paseo Exhacienda San Miguel, 52
Cuautitlán Izcalli
Estado de México, México
Tel. +55 16761811
e-mail: gabrielpacheco00@yahoo.com

Place and Date of Birth
Ciudad de México, México 12 January 1973

Published Titles
El pollito de la Avellaneda, Ed. Kalandraka, Spain
La llave de oro y otros cuentos, Cuentos completos IV Jacob y Wilhelm Grimm, Editorial Anaya Spain

Technique
Digital Computer

p. 122

Alessandra Panzeri

Address
Via Verdi, 18
23893 Cassago Brianza (LC), Italy
Tel. +39 333 4571053
Fax. +39 039 956150
e-mail: el.graf@tiscali.it

Place and Date of Birth
Lecco, Italy 18 September 1972

Art School Attended
Accademia di Brera, Milano

Published Titles
Ti prendo Ti prendo, Orecchio Acerbo, Roma

Technique
Collage, acrylic, computer graphic

p. 124

Yeon-Cheol Park

Address
#101-1803, Boramae Gabeul
151015 Apt., 1718 Sillim5-dong
Gwanak-gu, Seoul, Republic of Korea
Tel. +82 18 289 1702
Fax. +82 23 142 1180
e-mail: softfe@hanmail.net

Place and Date of Birth
Seoul, Republic of Korea 5 April 1970

Published Titles
Bogeyman is Coming, Sigongsa Co., Seoul

Art School Attended
Kingston University, U.K.

Technique
Printmaking, computer graphic

p. 126

Lena Pflüger

Address
Bei der Hopfenkarre, 2
22047 Hamburg, Germany
Tel. +49 40 89805923
e-mail: lanafloogan@yahoo.com

Place and Date of Birth
Leimen, Germany 30 December 1981

Art School Attended
HAW - Hamburg University of Applied Sciences

School Director
Dorothea Wenzel

Co-ordinator
Bernd Mölck-Tassel

Technique
Mixed media

▲ UNPUBLISHED ▲

p. 128

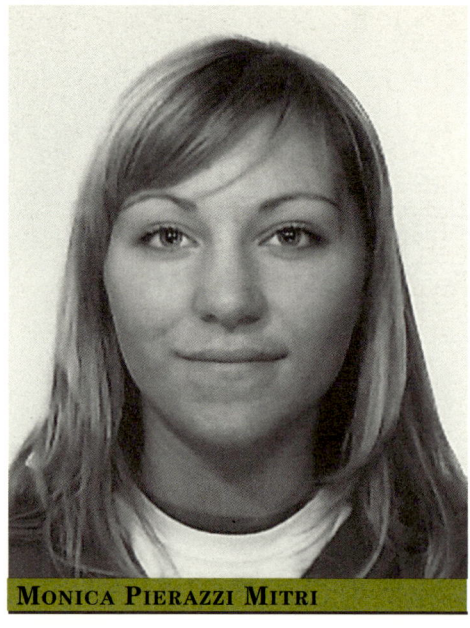

Monica Pierazzi Mitri

Address
Via Fabio Severo, 73/1
34100 Trieste, Italy
Tel. +39 340 5148063
e-mail: monica.lupul@gmail.com

Place and Date of Birth
Trieste, Italy 19 January 1983

Technique
Etching

▲ UNPUBLISHED ▲

p. 188

David Pintor

Address
Avda. Fonteculler, 50, 1°
15189 La Coruña, Spain
Tel. +34 676 381140
e.mail: davidpintor1975@yahoo.es

Place and Date of Birth
La Coruña, Spain 11 May 1975

Published Titles
Sobran as palabras, Xunta de Galicia
Suca, Everest
¿Qué sabemos do Día das Letras
 Galegas?, Xunta de Galicia
Aquilino pinta una nube y un
 camaleón, Combel
O libro dos xogos populares galegos, La
 Voz de Galicia
Dez por dous, Biblos
Hércules y Crunia, Kalandraka
Tito Longueirón, BD Banda
Historia de Román o bombeiro, Everest
O pequeno da familia fantasma, Sotelo
 Blanco
Cuentos en famiglia, Anaya

Technique
Ink, computer graphic

p. 130

Fulvia Pizzo

Address
Via Rucellai, 39
00058 Santa Marinella (RM), Italy
Tel. +39 328 9258267
e-mail: fulvia68@libero.it

Place and Date of Birth
Civitavecchia, Italy 6 February 1968

Technique
Acrylic on canvass

▲ U N P U B L I S H E D ▲

p. 132

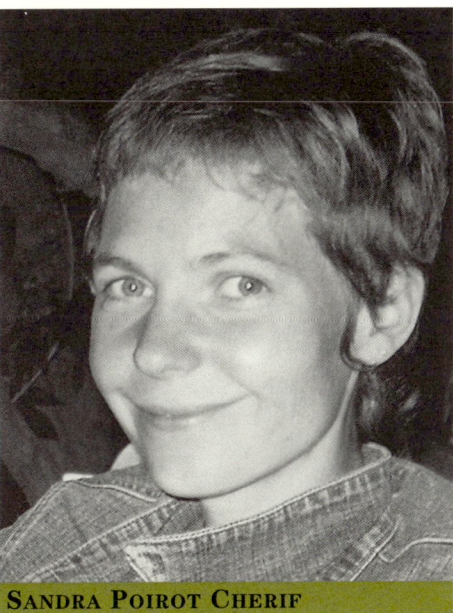

Sandra Poirot Cherif

Address
8, rue de la Paix
54000 Nancy, France
Tel. +33 618606968
Fax. +33 383321987
e-mail: sandra.poirotte@laposte.net

Place and Date of Birth
Nancy, France 2 March 1977

Published Titles
Dédé le dindon au pays de l'alphabet,
 Editions Albin-Michel, Paris
Le menteur, Editions Mango
Que sais-tu des rêves du lézard ?,
 Editions Magnard, Paris
L'eau de la lune, Editions du Minibus,
 Florange
Z. comme papa! Editions Didier, Paris

Technique
Acrylic, collage, oil pastels, fabric,
 pencil, gouache

p. 134

Clémence Pollet

Address
23, rue des Champs Elysées
94250 Gentilly, France
Tel. +33 146634302
e-mail: clem_ance@hotmail.com

Place and Date of Birth
Courbevoie, France 1 May 1985

Art School Attended
Ecole Supérieure Estienne

School Director
Mme Kunhmunch

Co-ordinator
Mr. Pourquié
Mr. Soularue

Technique
Watercolor, pen, collage, pastels

▲ U N P U B L I S H E D ▲

p. 136

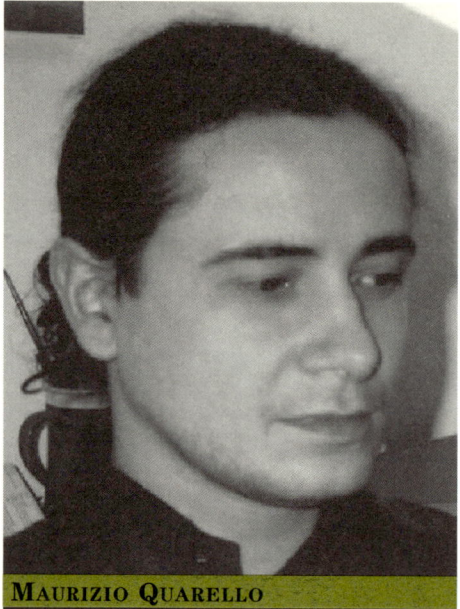

Maurizio Quarello

Address
109, Plešivecká
381 01 Český Krumlov, Czech Republic
Tel. +420 380711241
e-mail: maurizio@quarello.com

Place and Date of Birth
Torino, Italy 15 May 1974

Published Titles
Le voyage de la femme Eléphant, Editions Sarbacane, Paris
La petite fille qui avait perdu son visage, Editions Sarbacane, Paris
Anna fasst Mut!, Bohem Press, Zurich
Toni Mannaro jazz band in note di città, Orecchio Acerbo, Roma
Babau cerca casa, Orecchio Acerbo, Roma
La bruja rechinadientes, OQO Editora, Pontevedra
Mister Cuervo, OQO Editora, Pontevedra
Marizul que sueña que sueña que sueña…, OQO Editora Pontevedra
El Tragaldabas, OQO Editora Pontevedra
Dove va Crispino?, Fatatrac, Firenze
Nato straniero, Fatatrac, Firenze
1940-1945 Gioele fuga per tornare, Fatatrac, Firenze
Il viaggio di Luna, Edicolors, Genova
Una storia di magia, Edicolors, Genova
Ciccio il maiale quadrato, Falzea, Reggio Calabria
Tre cavalieri su una spider rossa, Falzea, Reggio Calabria
Le voci dei tam tam, dieci fiabe dall'Africa, collettiva di illustratori, Franco Panini, Modena

Technique
Mixed, acrylic

p. 138

Luigi Raffaelli

Address
Via Domenico Mazza, 54
61100 Pesaro, Italy
Tel. +39 0721 371854
e-mail: stomach@inwind.it

Place and Date of Birth
Pesaro, Italy 1 September 1974

Published Titles
Danzando nell'Ombra, Mondadori, Milano
Io e Jamaica, Mondadori, Milano
Oppi, Mondadori, Milano
Cyberattaque à la banque, Lang Edizioni
Venditempo, Orecchio Acerbo, Roma
Storie di un Dio pasticcione, Campanotto Ragazzi
Storie del terzo millennio, Campanotto Ragazzi
Mai contare sui Topi, Topipittori, Milano

Technique
Acrylic on paper

p. 140

Fabio Ramiro Rossin

Address
Via Carducci, 15
10090 Bruino (TO), Italy
Tel. +39 329 0249522
e-mail: fabioramirros@tiscali.it

Place and Date of Birth
Torino, Italy 12 March 1983

Technique
Acrylic, pen on canvas

▲ U N P U B L I S H E D ▲

Linda Rastatter

Address
Szépkilatas utca, 2
1121 Budapest, Hungary
Tel. +36 303344416
e-mail: rastatter@freemail.hu

Place and Date of Birth
Miskolc, Hungary 28 November 1983

Art School Attended
Moholy Nagy University of Arts and Design of Budapest

School Director
Gabor Kopek

Co-ordinator
György Pálfi

Technique
Acrylic

▲ U N P U B L I S H E D ▲

Piret Raud

Address
Pronksi, 6-46
10124 Tallinn, Estonia
Tel. +372 66 12 276
e-mail: piretraud@solo.delfi.ee

Place and Date of Birth
Tallinn, Estonia 15 July 1971

Published Titles
Keeruline lugu, Tiritamm, Tallinn
Kataleena isemoodi juuksed, Sinisukk, Tallinn
Kala Kõnnib jala, Varrak, Tallinn
Muusikaõpetus IV klassile, Avita, Tallinn
_hel viivul vikervalgel, Tiritamm, Tallinn
Maailm Sulelise ja Karvasega, Varrak, Tallinn
Eesti muinasjutud, Tiritamm, Tallinn
Pätu, Avita, Tallinn
Paula Sari, Tiritamm, Tallinn
Draakonid võõrsil, Tiritamm, Tallinn
Sookoll ja sisalik, Tiritamm, Tallinn
Kallis härra Q, Avita, Tallinn
Ernesto Küülikud, Tänapäev, Tallinn
Onu Volgi Värsiaabits, Eesti Entsüklopeediakirjastus, Tallinn
Dixi ja Xixi, Ilo, Tallinn
Sanna ja salakütid, Tänapäev

Technique
Indian ink., watercolour, pencil

Mandana Sadat

Address
11 bis, chemin des Taupiniaux
91120 Palaiseau, France
Tel. +33 01 60105348
e-mail: sadat.mandana@wanadoo.fr

Place and Date of Birth
Bruxelles, Belgium 21 May 1971

Published Titles
De l'autre côté de l'arbre, Grandir, Nîmes
Le jardin de Babaï, Grandir, Nîmes
Tarde de inverno, SM ediciones, México
Mon lion, Autrement jeunesse, Paris
Kodor, Syros, Paris
Cosas con plumas, Kokinos, Madrid
L'altro Paolo, Orecchio Acerbo, Roma

Technique
Mixed, computer

p. 148

Alessandro Sanna

Address
Via G. Puccini, 15
46030 Ostiglia (MN), Italy
Tel. +39 339 61 56 329
e-mail: alesanna@box.it

Place and Date of Birth
Nogara, Italy 10 October 1975

Published Titles
A sbagliare le storie, Emme Edizioni, Trieste
Hai mai visto Mondrian?, Edizioni Artebambini, Bazzano
Mostra di Pittura, Edizioni Corraini, Mantova

Technique
Indian Ink, watercolour

p. 150

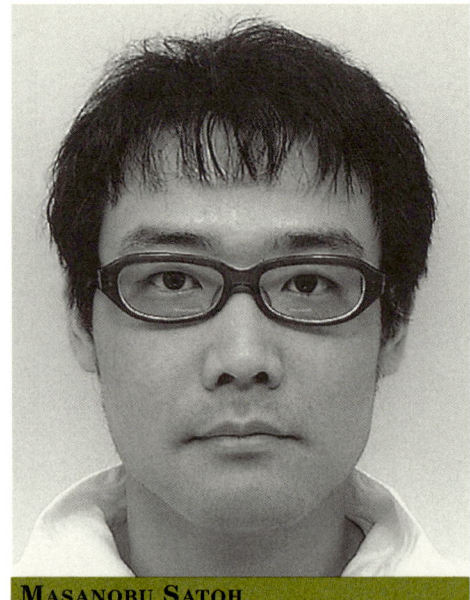

Masanobu Satoh

Address
1-41-11-301 Sangenjyaya Setagaya-ku
154-0024 Tokyo, Japan
Tel. +81 03 3412 9031
Fax. +81 03 3412 9031
e-mail: potu@aurora.dti.ne.jp

Place and Date of Birth
Tokyo, Japan 27 June 1972

Technique
Acrylic resin

▲ UNPUBLISHED ▲

p. 152

Amir Shaabanipour

Address
c/o Shabaviz Publishing Co.
No.2, Nouri Alley, Jomhouri Eslami Ave.,
Between Golshan St. and Bastan St.
13186 – 45163 Tehran, Iran
Tel. +98 21 6642 3995
Fax. +98 21 6642 7858
e-mail: shabaviz@sahabaviz.com

Place and Date of Birth
Fouman, Iran, 1978

Published Titles
Clever Rabbit and Mother magpie,
 Shabaviz Publishing Co., Tehran
A Rainbow of Shoes, Shabaviz
 Publishing Co., Tehran
The Fox, Shabaviz Publishing Co.,
 Tehran

Technique
Mixed

p. 154

Tomomi Shiozawa

Address
Syakujiidai 4-1-3-908
177-0045 Nerimaku, Tokyo, Japan
Tel. +81 3 3928 6641
Fax. +81 2 3928 6641
e-mail: tomobcn@hotmail.com

Place and Date of Birth
Saitama, Japan 1 December 1974

Technique
Watercolor, pen

▲ U N P U B L I S H E D ▲

p. 190

Annika Siems

Address
Erlenkam, 20
22087 Hamburg, Germany
Tel. +49 40 41541817
e-mail: annikasiems@gmx.de

Place and Date of Birth
Pinneberg, Germany 28 March 1984

Art School Attended
HAW - Hamburg University of Applied
Sciences

School Director
Dorothea Wenzel

Co-ordinator
Bernd Mölck-Tassel

Technique
Acryl, oil

▲ U N P U B L I S H E D ▲

p. 192

Marie Sommer

Address
44, rue St. Anne
75002 Paris, France
Tel. +33 06 07640926
e-mail: sommer@ensad.fr

Place and Date of Birth
Paris, France 5 September 1984

Art School Attended
ENSAD - Ecole Nationale Supérieure des Arts Décoratifs

School Director
Patrick Raynaud

Co-ordinator
Denis Perus

Technique
Etching

▲ **UNPUBLISHED** ▲

p. 156

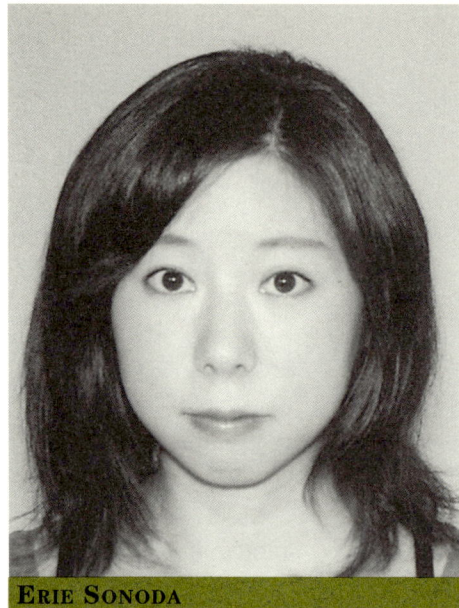

Erie Sonoda

Address
3-32 Kioi-cho Chiyoda-ku
102-0094 Tokyo, Japan
Tel. +81 3 3261 7539
Fax. +81 3 3261 7539
e-mail: erikuri@abox2.so-net.ne.jp

Place and Date of Birth
Vancouver, Canada 29 November 1981

Technique
Pencil, pastels

▲ **UNPUBLISHED** ▲

p. 142

Franki Sparke

Address
45, Molesworth St., Watson
2602 Canberra, Act, Australia
Tel. +61 02 62 411 008
e-mail: frankisparke@hotmail.com

Place and Date of Birth
Newcastle, Australia 26 June 1953

Technique
Stamped relief-print, gouache

▲ **UNPUBLISHED** ▲

p. 144

Jochen Stuhrmann

Address
Hoheluftchaussee, 128
20253 Hamburg, Germany
Tel. +49 0177 3687423
e-mail: jostuhrmann@gmx.de

Place and Date of Birth
Siegen, Germany 16 March 1976

Published Titles
Ernesto – Eine lange Reise auf kurzen Beinen, Bajazzo Verlag, Zürich

Technique
Acrylic on paper

Yoko Tanaka

Address
65, Arlington Dr. #3
91105 Pasadena, CA, USA
Tel. +1 323 717 5404
e-mail: yoko@yokotanaka.com

Place and Date of Birth
Tokyo, Japan 8 October 1968

Art School Attended
Art Center College of Design, Pasadena, CA

Published Titles
Theodosia and the Serpents of Chaos, Houghton Mifflin Company, Boston

Technique
Acrylic glazing

Ta-Yuan Tsai

Address
12 F-2 No 136, Jianmin Rd., Lingya District
80289 Kaohsiung City, Taiwan
Tel. +88 6 77114678
e-mail: pollock1966@yahoo.com.tw

Place and Date of Birth
Taiwan, 1 March 1966

Art School Attended
School of Visual Communication Design, National Kaohsiung Normal University

School Director
Chia-nana Tai

Co-ordinator
Yi-Xun Li

Technique
Watercolor, colored pencils

p. 162   *p. 164*   *p. 166*

Kouki Tsuritani

Address
495-1 Nishikawakura Yatsuomachi
939-2417 Toyama, Japan
Tel. +81 076 454 7024
Fax. +81 076 454 7024
e-mail: kouki4@mac.com

Place and Date of Birth
Tokyo, Japan 4 October 1967

Technique
Mezzotint

▲ U N P U B L I S H E D ▲

p. 168

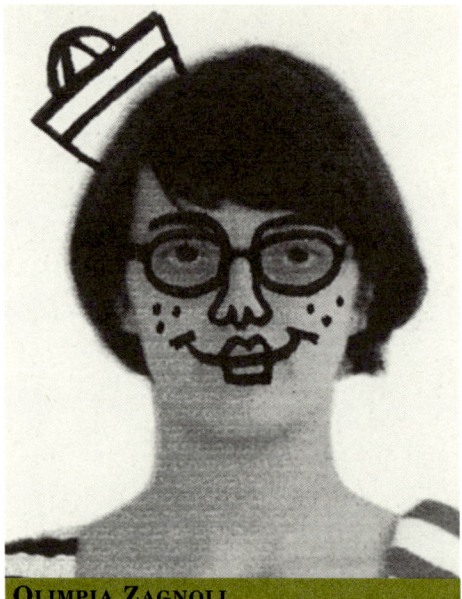

Olimpia Zagnoli

Address
V.le Coni Zugna, 34
20144 Milano, Italy
Tel. +39 347 7154986
e-mail: olimpia.zagnoli@gmail.com

Place and Date of Birth
Montecchio Emilia (RE), Italy 29 February 1984

Technique
Mixed media

▲ U N P U B L I S H E D ▲

p. 194

Pyotr Zhilichkin

Address
Narodnaya, 14, bld. 2
127018 Moscow, Russia
Tel. +7 095 912 08 99
Fax. +7 095 912 08 99
e-mail: grimm_copyrights@cite.com.tw

Place and Date of Birth
Russia, 1 February 1946

Published Titles
Life of the Plants, Drofa, Russia
My First Book about Nature, Drofa, Russia
The Life Cycles, Tormont, Canada
Fabre, Montessori, Korea
The Insects, Russia

Technique
Watercolor

p. 196

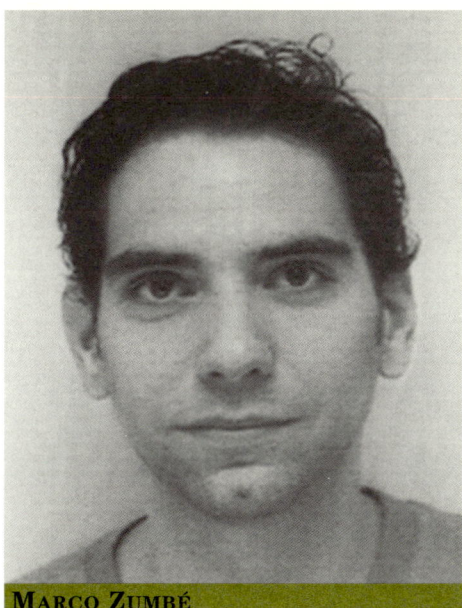

Marco Zumbé

Address
Am Elisabethgehölz
20535, Hamburg, Germany
Tel. +49 40 25 331 999
Fax. +49 40 25 331 999
e-mail: mzumbe@web.de

Place and Date of Birth
Colonge, Germany 6 April 1975

Art School Attended
HAW - Hamburg University of Applied Sciences

School Director
Dorothea Wenzel

Co-ordinator
Bernd Mölk-Tassel

Technique
Scratchboard, Photoshop

p. 170